Shall painting become the sordid drudgery of self representation of merely mortal man and perishing substances and not be elevated into its own sphere of invention and visionary conception? No, it shall not be so. Painting as well as poetry exists and exults in immortal thoughts.

– William Blake, 1805

Christopher Neve (1942–2024) was a painter and writer. His book *Unquiet Landscape: Places and Ideas in 20th-Century British Painting* (new edition, 2020), arose out of long talks with Ben Nicholson and other artists, and is published by Thames & Hudson.

IMMORTAL THOUGHTS

CHRISTOPHER NEVE

Foreword by
JOHN BANVILLE

with 29 illustrations

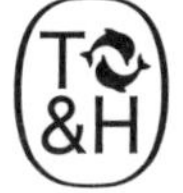

ON THE COVER: Rembrandt van Rijn, *Self-portrait, c.* 1628.
Oil on panel, 22.6 × 18.7 cm (9 × 7⅜ in., without frame).
Rijksmuseum, Amsterdam.

First published in the United Kingdom in 2023 by
Thames & Hudson Ltd, 6–24 Britannia Street, London WC1X 9JD

This paperback edition published in 2025

Immortal Thoughts: Late Style in a Time of Plague
© 2023 and 2025 Thames & Hudson Ltd, London

Text © 2023 Christopher Neve
Foreword (extract from 'Art at the Close') © 2023 John Banville
A longer version of this essay originally appeared in
The New Statesman

Designed by Dinah Drazin

EU Authorized Representative: Interart S.A.R.L.
19 rue Charles Auray, 93500 Pantin, Paris, France
productsafety@thameshudson.co.uk
interart.fr

A CIP catalogue record for this book is available from
the British Library

ISBN 978-0-500-29824-4
01

Printed and bound in the United Kingdom by Bell & Bain Ltd

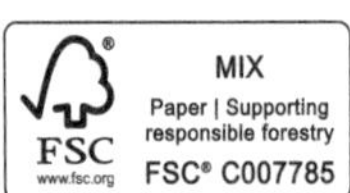

Contents

Foreword

Christopher Neve's *Immortal Thoughts* is a direct and conscious attempt to distil, by a passionate engagement with the work of some eighteen artists, the essence of art itself, or, rather, to approach as closely as possible the essential mystery which every true work of art embodies. It is rare indeed to encounter a book about art which is itself a work of art.

Neve writes about the lives and daily doings of his subjects with a novelist's freedom and intensity. His powers of empathy and evocation are prodigious. Again and again we are 'there', with Titian in Venice, with Rembrandt in Amsterdam, with Bonnard in Le Cannet on the Cote d'Azur. No less vivid are his descriptions of the glorious spring, summer and autumn of 2020, as the pandemic swept irresistibly westwards with its unsparing scythe.

A painter, Neve was born in 1942, and is therefore eligible to write out of personal experience on late style, 'that odd compound of thought beyond reason, when, in painting, the constraints of patronage, sharp eyesight and public approval are left behind'.

The opening chapter is on Cézanne, and specifically the watercolours which were among the painter's last works. Here we are presented for the first of many times with the 'indefinable subject' which will be Neve's quarry throughout, one that he will never track down, but whose lair, at least, he manages to locate.

As he entered upon old age, Cézanne's personal uncouthness, his 'rudeness, even crudity', became more and more an aspect of his work, 'because what he is looking for is not refinement but the absolute truth', that 'quite terrifying truth' which stands ever unrevealed behind the so-called ordinary. This is the paradox. The old painter is seeking 'a way to make the unseen visible', as Neve insists he managed to do. But how could he? Surely what art shows us, what it directs our gaze towards, is the 'essential mystery' which Neve locates at the heart of mundane reality.

The painter, and the painting, that address most tellingly the persisting theme of Neve's book are Velázquez and his sublime masterpiece, *Las Meninas*, a grave yet playful, not to say mischievous, group portrait centring on the five-year-old daughter of Philip IV of Spain and Queen Mariana, the infanta Margarita Teresa, who will die at the age of twenty-one after enduring seven pregnancies. This picture, one of the very greatest works in Western art, is at once luminous and shadowed. The more one looks at it, the more of itself it withholds. This is a part of its greatness.

All true works of art exist in a state of withdrawal, as Neve repeatedly acknowledges. This is why we return to these works again and again; it is why their newness never fades. To confront *Las Meninas* is to be in turn confronted, figuratively and literally. Of the eleven figures depicted, three look directly at the viewer. These are the infanta, the lovingly fashioned dwarf Maribárbola, and the painter himself, though he may have one eye on the painting before him on the easel.

What do their gazes convey? At most, a knowing absence. The world of the picture, Velázquez's amused eye informs us, is closed: we may not enter there, where time has no dominion, where the King and his consort are inconsequential phantoms, where Margarita Teresa will never become pregnant and will never die. 'In the end the picture is both heartbreakingly beautiful and a complete mystery.'

Neve's final chapter is his finest. Soutine is obviously one of his favourite painters, and here he celebrates him as the very definer of his subject: 'This, in the end, is what great late painting can be: the world reduced to a series of prodigious impulses, the revelation of the inner self intact, the chance taken to see the universe in a new light at the risk of failing utterly.'

John Banville

Introduction

There was only one idea that interested me then, which was to record all that had been omitted in previous books about late style.

When the plague began I went to a place in the country where I could write for a year and see nobody. I had the artists who are always in my head for company so I was never for a moment lonely. On starting to write about them I came to realize that what we had in common was the experience of producing late work. It was a curious fact that, while time lasted, there was time enough for everything.

Late style, that odd compound of thought beyond reason, when, in painting, the constraints of patronage, sharp eyesight and public approval are left behind. Part death, part memory, part intuition. A way of working that transcends technique and sets no store by the ability to finish. A willingness to take risks, to chance the arm. The urgent need to leave behind terms of reference and get to the heart of the matter without breaking off to explain.

There is a certain smudginess of handling, ambiguity and half-formed thought at the far end of painting, beyond knowing but not beyond recognition. Sometimes it belongs to great artists who continued working into extreme old age, like Michelangelo and Titian, and it is discernible sometimes in those who did not know that they were stopping, like Velázquez. Only very rarely do you see it in the late work of those whose output petered out long before they died, like Gwen John. I believe they all have something in common.

I have thought about this my whole life, but it is only now that it is almost too late that I dare to set it down. I am surrounded by death and have the opportunity to test my own against the deaths and last work of the artists I most admire. For this reason I shall juxtapose an account of the pandemic and the changing seasons in 2020 with my ideas on the business of painting.

There was also the figure of Time, a 17th-century allegorical sculpture which, until it became unsafe, had been fixed high up on the church tower of the local market town and was now set up in a far part of the garden. It was stone-grey and lichen-covered, life-sized, almost naked, with exaggerated features, extravagant beard and forelock and a beetling downward gaze. When I was not writing or growing vegetables I tried to repair its cracked skull, damaged arms and long, cadaverous, old man's torso.

In this way I not only had much to do and to write about as the plague crept nearer, but was even happy, except when the pain came, because it was a beautiful spring and hot weather and I was thinking about time.

I lived very simply, in rooms I had known as a child. The old wireless in its fretwork cabinet in the kitchen kept me abreast of the news, though I took care not to listen too often.

The unfolding drama did have a certain fascination. In England the prime minister caught the plague, as did some members of the royal family. The prime minister went into hospital for intensive care, and the very old Queen broadcast to the nation about suffering. Refugee centres and armies faced chaos. The plague spread rapidly through the slums of India. In Italy they started to put bodies on ice rinks because there were too many to bury. Homes for the elderly were left without enough staff to care for the residents trapped inside. Everywhere, the sick died alone because no one was allowed to visit them for fear of spreading the plague.

Where I was, fritillaries, cowslips, violets, primroses and daffodils were more prolific than ever. To the tiny scents of winter honeysuckle and witchhazel was added the smell of the small wild daffodil, pseudonarcissus, in the woods. Prolonged winter rain had indulged the fruit trees so that they bloomed inordinately. First the white Japanese cherry, Mount Fuji, then the pear with its red anthers, then the native cherry and the first plum blossom against the delicate blue of the unpolluted sky. There were no aeroplanes. The sky was exhilaratingly fresh and clear. There were no cars. Four times a day I would hear the horseman pass by in the empty lane. The evocative song of chaffinches was everywhere, the eggs in song thrushes' nests a wonderful blue. Goldcrests were in the pear blossom.

In Venice the canals reverted to Canaletto blue because there were no boats to churn up their sediment. Because there was no longer any space in which to bury the dead in New York, trenches were dug in public parks for use as temporary mass graves. All galleries and museums were closed and thieves broke in to help themselves. A great Titian exhibition, set up in London at the National Gallery, hung unvisited. Rough sleepers died in the streets. Zoos were deserted, the animals set free or abandoned to die after using the last of their feed.

  Before many days had passed, great numbers of doctors and nurses began to die.

The cuckoo arrived, and then the swallows. Ceanothus opened. Bluebells, periwinkles, anemones. A sadder and a lovelier spring.

Cézanne's Last Watercolours

Now come with me in memory to the late summer of 1904 in Aix-en-Provence.

By now the sun has exhausted Place Jeanne d'Arc and the fountain has dried up. Shop awnings have faded and a row of worn-out cab horses, tormented by flies, wait in the shade on the Cours Mirabeau. Poor men, out of work and at a loose end, wear the remains of military uniforms. There are the smells of leather, garlic and sweat. At midday the sound of plates and forks behind closed shutters. Six or seven children hang around in the dust in Place de l'Hôtel-de-Ville, their shadows short, hoping something might happen, but nothing does. There is nothing doing. The butcher closes. The abbé, whom Cézanne dislikes, leaves the cathedral by a side door and walks round the corner into rue Jacques de la Roque.

All these places are there in the pictures. The Jas de Bouffan, Cézanne's father's house, is shut up, its avenue of dispirited chestnut trees and acacias shading the drive and what remains of the rectangular water-tank holding a green reflection. His father had started out selling rabbit skins for hats, later transforming himself into a prosperous banker and living on a provincial bourgeois scale. There was much that Cézanne needed to conceal from him: his failure to pursue law studies in Paris, his illegitimate son, his eventual marriage to Hortense, who preferred ice-cream to conversation. As a concession, his father had let Cézanne paint on the walls between the tall windows in the dining-room, and sat reading the paper for an awkward portrait or two. Paulin Paulet, a gardener at the Jas de Bouffan, had posed as one of Cézanne's card players at five francs a time in the 1890s. But now, after a tussle with his devout elder sister following their mother's death, the house has been sold and Cézanne seldom goes there. It stands with its blueish shutters closed in the afternoons, left alone with the deafening chorus of cicadas, the hot grass unscythed.

Instead, on the proceeds, Cézanne has found a perfectly good room or two on rue Boulegon in the town, where the old house-keeper, Madame Manuelle, keeps him in order and feeds him. His wife and child are in Paris. He prefers to be alone so that he can get on. He is cantankerous and feels ill. In his letters he refers often to his great age, which is only sixty-four. The museum at Aix has turned down his offer to give them some pictures. Cézanne calls Henri Pontier, the director of Aix Museum, 'that dirty brute'. Now his one idea is to die painting, always with the sense that what he has sought all his life is at last almost within reach: some discovery or realization of what it is like to make the sensation of seeing into a truthful series of marks on the canvas.

He has a skylight put into the roof at 23 rue Boulegon so that he can see what he is doing, then changes his mind and sketches out an idea for a purpose-built studio clear of the new development where the town stretches northwards up the slope on the Chemin des Lauves. Here, in a big first-floor studio, he can set out the few battered objects he has always hauled around with him to paint: the double-fronted desk, bow-fronted table, the familiar red jug, cream dish, blue and white bowl, his studio skulls. A few steps up the road gives him the long, blue view across the speckled landscape towards the distant railway viaduct and the hunched shoulder of the mountain. And from the short terrace beneath his windows he can look down on the roofs and towers of Aix.

But his new studio does not mean that Cézanne discontinues infesting the landscape. Far from it. He has already rented a hut in the scrubby woodland not far from Le Château Noir in which he can lock up his easel and box of paints. The weather is stifling and he enters into a long-running, ill-tempered arrangement with a carter called Carrafanq whose job it becomes to collect him in the early mornings, before the heat is too great, and take him by horse and cart to his various painting sites – out by the bridge of Trois-Sautets, where he bathed as a boy with his friend Zola, or to the overgrown quarry at Bibémus – then bring him back again in the evenings. Latterly he has taken to going in the evenings to the Gour de Martelly district, south of the town, where there is some shade on the little path that leads to Montbriand. They argue about what seems to Cézanne the exorbitant rate of three francs that Carrafanq charges to do all this, and he is sometimes laid off. However, it is in Cézanne's nature to pick quarrels, and Carrafanq is always eventually laid on again. When Émile Bernard, one of several young painters who have begun to take an interest in Cézanne's work, comes on the train to visit him, he takes two or three photographs of the painter at work outdoors. Or is he only pretending to work? What we see is what remains of the passionate, black-bearded figure of the early self-portraits: a bent, elderly man in hot clothes, wearing something like a homburg hat.

So you think you know what painting is? This is the man who thinks it is entirely drawing, who has taken offence at Monet, and whose stubborn persistence is the same quality he admires in his old peasant friend Camille Pissarro. Cézanne is conservative in his views, hates the new liturgy and has suffered lifelong from an inability to reconcile the two sides of his nature, as the rest of us do. On the one hand, angst. On the other, a longing for order. But perhaps you know all this, the rapes and violence that he drew when he was young and the restraint he imposed by vigorous scrutiny as he got older. When you speak to him, he is deliberately uncouth. This rudeness, even crudity, a social awkwardness, is visible even now in the drawings or in the restrained violence of his handling as a painter, because what he is looking for is not refinement but the absolute truth. And this insistence on the truth makes him irritable. It is, and always has been, uphill work. In the process it has given us some of the most marvellous and grandest pictures we shall ever be fortunate enough to see.

But it has not given him, or us, one thing which is the all but indefinable subject of this essay about his watercolours. I feel the load of a responsibility here because, in seriousness, I must not misrepresent his integrity.

When it comes to the watercolours, you are up against a great mystery. Like the St John Passion, they take place in the past tense. A man in old age can begin to wonder if the account he has always given of himself is really true, or whether he has not somehow replaced the original narrative. If so, is his invented history more true than the real? Is it a heightened form? Cézanne used watercolour off and on for forty years before this, much as he used drawing, to approach an idea. He never showed a watercolour. He used it with reticence, touching the page as little as possible, leaving much of the sheet empty. I once met Christopher Logue, the dissident English poet, on a train from the coast and we talked for an hour about a poem he had always wanted to write which would have nothing in the middle of it but an inexplicable idea. It would be complete but somehow contain at its centre nothing you could mention or define. Cézanne's fragmentary and intermittent watercolours remind me of this.

By the time he is old, everything in the watercolours remembered from the past is prophetic of the future. That superb bather diving into the water from the 1860s (Venturi 818) has the back of the Greek sculpture he had so often drawn in the Louvre. Does the future resemble the past? The work of memory, Walter Benjamin suggested, is to read oneself backwards, collapsing time. But as he gets older, does not Cézanne begin to think that behind the ordinary is some quite terrifying truth which is unrevealed? If so, do the watercolours try repeatedly to tell some secret that won't go into them? A simulacrum. A copy of something that does not exist. He has tried for years to come up with something on this topic, which is absolutely not visited by the resoundingly solid resolutions of the oil paintings. It torments him. As he says, he sees the promised land but fears that he may not after all have time to enter it.

At this level the watercolours are oddly feverish. For example, the *Three Women Bathers* and *La Lutte d'amour* of 1875–76 (Venturi 898 and 897). Too sane, he is saying to himself. Too sane. Much madness is good sense except to others. 'It is the mistral in him,' as Cézanne himself said of Puget. 'It is what makes the marble vibrate.'

When Maurice Denis and Ker Roussel come to find Cézanne in Aix in January 1906, they are told by the maid in his rooms that he is attending high mass at Saint-Sauveur. They meet him coming out of the cathedral. 'Manteau gris-vert, veston et gilet tachés, les mains sales, la tête nue.' Grey-green cloak, stained jacket and waistcoat, dirty hands, bare head. Cézanne, wherever he went, always carried with him a photograph of the three voluptuous linked naiads from the foreground of Rubens's *Arrival of Marie de Medici at Marseilles*. Within him, always the turmoil.

And then, like Dostoevsky, he sees a way to make the unseen visible. The beautiful, widespread touches that before have established a flute-note of musical colour at widely spaced intervals in the watercolours, like little patches of green shade, can be made not just to join up but to lie with simplicity one upon another.

Old Vallier, his gardener and odd-job man at the Les Lauves studio, sits patiently on a kitchen chair, half in and half out of the shade of a tree, and Cézanne begins to say of him: well, there is that but there is also, at the same time, perhaps this. In the oil paintings these alternative views accumulate in increasingly congested dark paint. In the watercolours they are lucid, limpid.

It is getting late, his diabetes is worse, but in drawings of a bottle, some apples or the back of a chair in the studio, or a row of pears and kitchen utensils interspersed on a shelf, Cézanne can begin to say that, for himself, two or more truths can be stated *at the same time*. He is not dogmatic. Although of course he has strong views and can never quite bring himself to speak against Impressionism, people notice that he often has a way of prefacing remarks about art by saying 'For me, such and such.' *Pour moi*. Long afterwards, Madame Cézanne said to Matisse: 'You understand, he didn't know what he was doing.'

But of course he does, and this is how it is in the watercolours. Two or more possibilities can be set down simultaneously as if to contain the essential mystery. Even Mont Sainte-Victoire, so long observed in watercolour by isolated patches, can be seen from Les Lauves by 1906 in a succession of overlapping brushmarks. In this way I think he at last begins to catch at something that has eluded him so far. I will not try to define it. It is not atmosphere and not, certainly not, sentiment. But suppose you were to look at Sainte-Victoire from the Route du Tholonet, or at Aix from the Les Lauves terrace in the heat or when the heat has at last gone. What you don't see is the shimmer, the smallest air-blue interval between objects and between the painter and the view which might conceivably be discernible in watercolour because, unlike oil, it is transparent.

The weather did for Cézanne: he was caught in a thunderstorm when out painting and brought home to rue Boulegon in a laundry cart. He was put to bed but developed pneumonia and died alone, Madame Cézanne having been detained in Paris by a fitting with her dressmaker. But this did not matter because, not long before, Cézanne had painted the view of Saint-Sauveur from his terrace, with lemons on the tree, in watercolour, thus solving everything.

*Then in England the government told the army, 'Build hospitals!'
Emergency hospitals on an enormous scale were quickly built all
over the country. The plague paid no heed to the spring.*

*English churches were closed and locked at Easter for the first time
since King John's disagreement with the Pope in the 13th century.*

And the beaches and palmy promenades of the Côte d'Azur
were empty, the sea running in and turning over with a lisp in
near-silence.

Bonnard's Last Four Paintings

It is a baleful business going up the steep street in the heat in Le Cannet on the Côte d'Azur to call on Bonnard in 1946, I can tell you.

He seems weak. He is seventy-nine. A melancholic with no vitality. He has no appetite and keeps his sunhat on indoors. He says little. His wife, Marthe, died five years ago. He has locked her room. Never goes into it. Her long legs and narrow back, yellowish when naked, are no longer reflected in the mirror or in the bath. She did not so much grow old as simply cease. The time is over, you see. The time of small pet dogs on chairs and garden furniture. Visitors in striped and spotted clothes. Trays of fruit and pâtisserie, *tartes aux fraises* well glazed, and *petits choux* in great profusion on red cloths or on white when sun poured in through the dining-room window to give cups and bowls their blue and violet shadows. All that has finished, or is on the very point of finishing, when you get there.

Pierre Bonnard looks at his face and narrow shoulders in the shaving mirror and sees without a doubt that he is an absence, an absence with worry lines on the forehead, weak eyes behind round glasses, a thin apology for a moustache. His face is pale as greenish milk against the bright light.

All life is at the foot of the hill where twin ribbons of traffic wind their way, glittering, along the coast road in the direction of the Grande Corniche. The Côte d'Azur has become crowded. The Americans are back, with the benefit of the exchange rate, and the pre-war bars and casinos have reopened. Here are the beaches, Plage de la Garoupe, where the ever youthful and glamorous Chou Valton and Lolo Burki bronzed themselves; also the villas rented by the very rich Gerald and Sara Murphy and the Scott Fitzgeralds in pre-war summers. Picasso, having hurried back to the coast from Paris, is installed courtesy of the municipality at Château Grimaldi in Antibes. He sends crates of oranges to Matisse, who is working as usual at Nice and Vence. Picasso does not think much of Bonnard. There were always antipathies. Renoir sent Matisse away with a flea in his ear. Léger is at Biot, Chagall at Vence. All European high modernism has been, or will be, here. Ozenfant, Zadkine, Arp, Van Doesburg, Delaunay, Le Corbusier. De Staël will paint some exuberantly optimistic pictures and then kill himself jumping from the cliff at Antibes. It is twenty-five years since Renoir, brushes strapped to his crippled hands, finished at Cagnes and Magagnosc. Now there is the tearing-calico noise of Bugatti exhaust, or Hispano-Suiza as Lartigue makes his way to Nice, and Van Dongen has painted himself, after a fancy-dress party, as Neptune. Compared to all this, Bonnard is very quiet.

You drag yourself up the hill. A gate in the wall. The name of the house, Le Bosquet, in italic writing. It is a modest villa, built by a speculator in 1924 and bought by Bonnard in 1925 when Le Cannet, now a suburb of Cannes, was a village with a village shop. There is a garden, enlarged by Bonnard's purchase of some neighbouring ground, some palms and fruit trees and a pink path which follows the slope to the winding Saigne drainage canal. Across to the left you can look out at the Îles de Lérins, and westwards over the rooftops there is an extensive view to the Esterel mountains.

Now Bonnard's elderly maid, Louie, opens the door to you. She wears a starched apron and is bursting with laughter. Her plump hands are folded on her stomach. You are to come in. M. Brassaï, whose photographs M. Bonnard much admires, was here yesterday and M. Bonnard hardly said a word to him, would not let him take a photograph except of his back view, was most reserved in fact. But he will like to see *you*. He is painting in the dining-room. You are to go through.

So this is how things stand at the villa Le Bosquet, as Bonnard's last summer is coming to an end.

Before I go on, I will try to remind you of the colour of his paintings without using any coloured adjectives. I have a reason.

Two children and some women in a boat. A closed-up house among trees. Flowers in a field with a distant church. Marthe washing herself with a sponge. A bowl of peaches. A new hat with a big bow on it. Marthe in a bedroom in the afternoon. Some boats at low tide. Some goats and a distant village. Some pots on a terrace with distant mountains. A beach and some bathers. A jug of poppies. A road sloping downhill between buildings. A hot afternoon on a lawn. A steam yacht and evening sky. The Mediterranean. A wicker chair with a cat near it. Someone who once played the piano in a room. Speckled wallpaper.

Now think of the drawings for these. They are on scraps of paper, on the pages of a diary, in little notebooks and on paper bags, done often as not with a fuzz of round hatching or swarms of dots, with a bluntish pencil. Long ago in the old days of the Nabis they used to be formal, these drawings, like little posters, but for a long time now they have become the beautiful, warm, incidental accompaniment to the pleasures of life, ways of putting a line round the shade of trees, the smell of books, the impress of letters on a table. The line does not have to define these things. It just hatches the soft shadow of where they are, the hum left in the air by an open window, a pile of fruit, a row of beach tents and a strip of sand, so that they can be referred to later. They are reminders on soft paper of what it felt like to see them rather than a map of their too particular attributes. Their personalities rather than their appearances.

And it is a wonderful thing to watch, this affectionate, scribbled record of the world accruing quite quickly and with such humanity on the disaffected page. The pencil lands on it and jots it wonderfully down in case such a small and transient episode as the edge of a table, a row of trees standing on their shadows, or an evening sky after a spring day outside Paris in the Île-de-France should somehow get away, or a barge go past the Quai de Montebello unobserved. Rolls of shadow, smudges and blinks of light and a few figures on a road are of consequence in a quick drawing after all, without any telling why. This is what Bonnard does by looking around him, by looking with the pencil moving. Not that it has to be complete. It is something continual, a process, the soft pencil moving much as the gardener moves the hoe, keeping chaos at bay. On the page the faint smoke of dark and light makes sense and the little memories add up.

All that may be the pretext but it is decidedly not the event, the plot but not the story.

You go in. (It is the dining-room, remember.) The room is empty. Nobody in it. The table has been pushed aside against the wall and it has colours and brushes on it, a palette, bottles and jars. The pleasant smell of linseed oil is in the room, and a rectangle of sunlight lies across the carpet. There are three chairs and a radiator. Discreet floral wallpaper. Audible across the passage, Louie drops something metal in the kitchen. A colander? The time is about half past three. Bonnard *is* in the room though the room remains empty. He has been standing behind the door. He does not want to talk, clearly does not wish his work to be interrupted.

And now you have the great good fortune to observe him, as you might observe a shy animal. He is taller than you expect, fairly tall and thin. There is space enough for him to stand, stooping, between the table and the wall. And that is where you see him mix colours and walk unsteadily across the room with a loaded brush. 'This,' he would no doubt say if he wanted to talk, 'is what I do. It is all I know how to do, and have always done. Not so much a habit as an impulse, you understand. And my only need.' He lifts the brush, deciding where to place the colour and in which painting. Because now you are privileged to see the slight secret of how Bonnard's last four pictures are done. He has put four rectangles of unstretched canvas on the dining-room wall, tacked up using drawing pins in the flocked wallpaper. Each of the four paintings is a different size and already quite well advanced: a view across the rooftops of Le Cannet, a dining-table picture, a still life with a basket of fruit, and a small picture of an almond tree in blossom.

On those rare occasions when he talks about painting, he is known to use the beautiful word *nourrisant*. Each picture is established, unconstrained by a stretcher, and what he will do now over a period of weeks is to nourish them with colour. He shuffles back to the table and assiduously fishes out a brush-tip of cerulean blue and works it into some citron, then some rose and eau-de-Nil, testing the values and timbres on a corner of the open palette as he goes, like a chef tasting *sauce ravigote*.

It is no pleasure feeling old and ill. When he was young the pictures were witty and surprising, oddly Japanese, liable to pitch an off-kilter view, infested with cabhorses and pet animals and the asymmetrical areas of open space that had first given Lautrec the idea to try posters. In those days it was Paris and the Île-de-France, its gravel gardens and parasols, and the willows on the point of the Île de la Cité, that had got into his decorative panels. And sometimes, when the apartment shutters were closed, the rooms contained only wallpaper, siesta wallpaper like fungal pondlife, in which you could barely see to thread a needle and a figure wearing the same dots on a print dress was invisible. But for the last twenty years, since he came to Le Bosquet, the far brighter light of the Midi and the lavender and mauve of his evening view of the Esterels have ripened his palette like a peach left on a windowsill. There is even more brightness in the paintings than in the garden, more even than where a sail waits for no breeze at all off Cap d'Antibes.

He recrosses the room. There is to be a large retrospective of his work in New York in September next year. He does not care. For out of this apparently timid, apparently undernourished man comes, touch by touch, mix by mix, dab by dab, the most ravishing apotheosis of indescribably beautiful late colour.

Did I tell you that by this time many thousands of people had died of the plague in Russia, where news of it had been suppressed, the authorities denying any knowledge of it? And the European economy came close to collapse for the first time since 1709. (In that year there was so great a frost that the Baltic Sea froze over, making it possible to ride a horse from Denmark to Sweden. All crops died and nothing would grow.)

Now almost nothing could be made, bought or sold. Paper money was contaminated. There was a fear of passing it from hand to hand because its spiteful surfaces contained the terrors of breathlessness and extinction. All round the world, especially around Australia, laden ships began to rust away in miles of ships' graveyards with starving crews marooned on them.

And here the apple blossom was opening from red buds to pink and white against the cloudless blue sky, and the first of the tortoiseshell and red admiral butterflies with their bright red stripes were in profusion. Ceanothus and bee-filled rosemary pumped out more blue in the afternoon sun than you would think possible.

Titian

Venice, June 1576. Titian is eighty-seven or eighty-eight. Narrow, bearded face, black gown, clawlike hands. There is about to be a plague here too, one that will kill a third of the population of Venice: about 70,000 dead, so many in fact that the death barges will call each morning, bobbing beneath the windows on the Grand Canal, for the corpses to be passed down to them, for all the world as if they were doing no more than collecting refuse. But for now, the city is scintillating. From Titian's palazzo, up near the Biri Grande, he can, even with old eyes, see the foothills of the Alps forty miles away. He writes letters about money, bothers people for contracts, chases up late creditors, paints over old canvases. When he speaks in commonplaces he seems in the grip of high emotion, as if behind the ordinary is some terrifying truth. He will not paint until he has to, does not even feel like painting until he begins.

But I think I invent him, make him up as an old man, so long has he been in my head. From the letters I have him down as a thrower of tantrums, a hurler of insults, one who creates mayhem, because who will go with him in the making of art when we cannot know a fraction of what he knows, and he, to himself, is the other? In the late work there used to be a way to get home. Look at the Lagoon. Not a trace of the approaching plague is on it where the fine vessels go about. Titian is the only person of all that 70,000 whom the city elders will allow to have a funeral despite the risks of infection. He is buried in the pink and lofty Frari, the noble Franciscan church of S.

Maria Gloriosa, in which his wife Celia, soon to die in childbirth at the time he paints it, is the Madonna in his miraculous Pesaro altarpiece.

Is it true that only in old age, as Delacroix says, the artist becomes the painter he should have been all along? Is painting an old man's art? So far, Titian's miraculous late style has lasted fifteen years.

Supposing, tomorrow, you were to take your courage in both hands and go up the hill in Naples to stand in front of his blood-red picture of Pope Paul III and his cringing, subversive grandsons. A terrifying picture. Titian, by this time (1546), fears nobody. He is not so much painting the Pope as laying bare, for his own reasons, what most interests him about his psychological situation. The foxy old Pope, in his late seventies, is thought to have said that the behaviour of his grandsons would be the death of him, and Titian knows a great deal about this from his own situation. Look at the ambiguous passage on the red tabletop, where he has altered the position of the Pope's right hand three times and somehow managed to arrive at a partly botched solution that incorporates all three versions of it. In this picture you can see a mighty painter at work, responding, improvising, changing his mind, doing what he always does on the way to a state that is unresolved, unfinished, yet hinting at a thrilling possible solution. The past, as Charles Lamb says, which is everything, is nothing. And the future, which is nothing, is everything. And yet, in painting, it is all a gamble. Francis Bacon suggested that Picasso did not need to gamble because he was gambling all day. No one is so old that he does not expect to live another year and, disregarding exhaustion and loss, Titian works out of chance and intuition towards a kind of exuberance, much as conversations consist of things we do not say.

Titian's house is hard to find: in the parish of San Canciano, facing onto the Lagoon in the direction of Murano. He has lived there since 1531. Does he not find that sometimes he works best on those days when he does not work, when he is thinking? What it is to be human! Begin, not with the fact of love, but with the state of mind which exists afterwards, when the world is transformed. I had a dog once that was starving because of a liver complaint. It was supposed to eat nothing but special food. For a long time it was practically a skeleton. Seeing that it was going to die anyway, I gave it all the food that it was supposed never to touch. How cheerful it became, and how fat, before it died. You may as well paint like that. The strict order of events often interrupts a narrative. Now, in old age, Titian is always coming up with solutions for which he was trying when younger. There is no point in lamenting your lack of muscle as you get old. It is knowledge you need, not muscle. False memory soon fills the vacuums in true memory. Why not raise a monument to amnesia and forget where you put it?

I think it is possible, when I look at late Titian, that he is working off a combination of nerves and unconscious memories, an inexhaustible store of memory outside of time. The unconscious relinquishes nothing, and nothing is forgotten. Nothing, as Freud says, is brought to an end. He speaks of traces. It is necessary to be very bold. Without great daring there is no beauty. Titian knows somehow to be beyond himself, exercising a breadth of handling that is incomparable, so that he is frequently accused of leaving pictures unfinished. There was a nasty moment when even Philip II of Spain seemed about to turn pictures down on the grounds that they were incomplete.

It is a curious quality, this apparent failure to finish, which extends to everything he paints. In a strange way, it is not important what his subject is, who or what he paints, by this time. The incomparable handling, which is true painting, is impalpable. It is nerves. It is done through and through and with apparent simplicity, as if he is in some sort of trance and does not breathe the air we breathe or feel much consciousness of what he is doing. Much later, Degas says: only when he no longer knows what he is doing does the painter do good things. And Cézanne says something similar about not stopping to think. Then there is a mysterious bridge put in place between the spirit in the picture and the viewer.

I dread talking about Titian's final way of painting. We have, as is well known, something very like a short film, which is his nephew Palma Giovane's description of him painting when Titian was about seventy. Palma does not show us much that we cannot see in the pictures. The vigorous red underpainting, the impulsive working up of high-toned areas using white lead, the ruthless demolitions and substitutions made with a broad brush as one part of the painting needs hastily to be changed to re-relate it to changes elsewhere. The constant drawing in colour. But one thing Palma does tell us that cannot be seen in the pictures is that Titian very often sets them aside when they are half done and does not look at them. And then – the telling remark – when Titian eventually does look at them again, he stares at them critically, 'as though they were mortal enemies', prior to setting about them, to remodel them, 'like a surgeon'.

It is a strange fact how many of the great Venetian artists lived to be old men. Tintoretto, seventy-six. Guardi eighty-one. Longhi eighty-three. Longhena eighty-four. Giovanni Bellini eighty-six. Da Ponte eighty-eight. Sansovino ninety-one. One half of Titian, now that he is in his late eighties, is already dead. Most of his best friends are dead: Aretino, the pornographer, who died laughing at an obscene joke about his own sister; Sansovino; and Zuccato, the mosaicist.

See Titian going about in Venice, the great man, the most celebrated and famous of all artists, to whom all the most important sitters in Europe have come for forty years to be painted. Yet in truth he is all that is left. Now his way of painting is sometimes to soften tones with a handful of dust. He is an avaricious old man, used to smudging oil paint with his hands. His son, Orazio, lives with him. Titian still has a flourishing studio and a large family. Nine grandchildren. There is his daughter Emilia. His second daughter, Lavinia, who died two years ago, had six children. His life is playing out well.

Death said to him once, 'Before you go, would you like to be reminded of anything?' And I like to think that he would have asked to see that sleeve, the sleeve now in the National Gallery in London, in a picture which Rembrandt came across in a dealer's house in Amsterdam in the 1630s and never got over, *Portrait of Gerolamo Barbarigo* (*c.* 1510). It is odd that artists, long after the event, can remember very well painting a particular passage. In life's dream, Titian will make a good end and return through madness, love and injustice to a silence in which brushstrokes, dabs, splits, softnesses, plumpnesses, grooves, creases, become both material and paint in that miraculously beautiful padded blue silk sleeve.

Now take a much later passage, like pregnant Callisto's stomach in the *Diana and Callisto* (1556–59, owned jointly by the National Galleries of Scotland and London), in which Titian uses chance to get at a controlled-looking result. It is only when your subconscious is working well and you have practised a great deal that you can hope to do this. It is as if surprise has taken over intention, and a random brushstroke reactivates a picture that has stuck. Titian knows very well that you can pile up facts but that they will not be entirely true until there is an ambiguity. Has he painted it once and then, using the same paint and some of the same drawing, somehow moved the whole passage sideways and restated it truthfully rather than factually? Often he begins to paint part of a form which he cannot see, as well as the side nearest to him. Is it not already waiting to happen in the man with the blue sleeve, where the full face seems about to move round the sharp profile? And, most wonderfully, it shows itself when, having drawn Diana from the side with her breast in profile, he paints her simultaneously from the back in *Diana and Actaeon*.

Anatomical accuracy jettisoned quite simply in favour of the truth. A breathtakingly beautiful reflex. As he gets older, this dash makes his whole world move. See the late *Rape of Europa* (1560–62, Isabella Stewart Gardner Museum, Boston) and *Death of Actaeon* (1559–75, National Gallery, London). Such a burstingly free hand and lively imagination.

But he has a crabbed appearance and for years has enjoyed making himself out to be much older than he is. Some people will do this, as if to point up the difference between their inner and outer lives. Like Cézanne, Titian started referring to himself as old in letters when he was under sixty. When he was sixty-seven, he once said he was eighty-five. When he was seventy-three, over eighty. And this when his painting was approaching its most miraculously vital. In fact he avoided all the incurable illnesses which, during his seventies, were carrying off friends and relations all round him. His nerve is not shaken. Venice is ruled by extremely old men. What Titian remembers better than anything is an instinctual way to paint, almost with violence.

And now I will try to say it in Venetian dialect to the dolorous slow beat of the great bell, the Marangona, which has sounded for six centuries in St Mark's campanile, because I can think of no other way of discussing something so mysterious, so wonderfully beyond words as Titian's last paintings, which raise the whole question of what painting can do or be. Around him, as he paints, remember the smells of mud and incense, fish and velvet. The melancholy, shimmering, translucent city in shallow, opaque water, lying crookedly in a kind of trance. A place of voluptuous materials and inexhaustible treasures as well as delight and sadness, surrounded by cruelly malarial islands on which cough the dying and insane.

First, but as no more than a clue, what seems to be his technique:

Titian's astounding energy, though he seems half dead. Broad brushstrokes. A hinting at big forms with freedom and economy.

High finish in some areas and only the most rudimentary indications in others, as if, having roughly established the position of Actaeon's leg or of some dogs, he has gone off to lunch.

Fast drawing with broken brushstrokes over underlying expanses of warm, reddish colour. By now he knows so much about how we see that he can trick us into recognizing forms without having to draw them in. A few patches of spontaneous marking will imply the remainder.

A preference for rough canvas and impatience with primer, which has the effect of unifying and interconnecting all parts of a picture via its texture.

A readiness to leave underdrawing in view and an acceptance of thin underlying statements.

A way of using the nap of the canvas that deposits paint only on the top surfaces of its weave.

No great enthusiasm for gesso, but an aptitude with rich glazes made using walnut oil.

All this amounts to a method of painting of such verve, sensuousness and immediacy that it works on you as high agitation.

Then, last, *sunt lacrimae rerum*, there are the tears of the world, you begin to realize something else.

It is unnaturally hot today. Occasional lightning behind Giudecca. Plagues have always approached up the Adriatic under the sails of traders. Six weeks and two days from now, Titian will be dead. He *is* his late style. Oil paint has become, with him, analogous to human flesh. It enters wounds. Brushstrokes cut and flay, scald and drown without mercy until it is necessary to look away. He is part of his own tragedy. Many of the late pictures are in some way violent – *The Flaying of Marsyas* (1570–76, Kroměříž, Czech Republic), *The Crowning with Thorns* (1576, Alte Pinakothek, Munich), *The Rape of Europa* and *S. Sebastian* (1570–72, Hermitage, St Petersburg), the unfinished *Pietà* (1575–76, Accademia, Venice). Their victims are twisted into the pictures' great schemes as parts of the human tragedy. Life is violent, and he paints it violently as if to restate the fact. Old subjects are revisited with greater urgency. Matter and spirit combust together. The anguish of human existence is transcended by his handling, the marvellous unity. He hazards marks and then follows them into what he remembers.

I wonder, in the late work, is there not a profound sense of something already done, as if the remembering part of the old painter's brain is somehow engaged in the wrong tense, as if the strong and peculiar smell of a particular herb comes to him out of the future and not from the past? The fluid medium stirs and the pictures come violently about. Hazard. Chance. Intuition. These paintings are far beyond reason, have been realized almost before our eyes in a rush of sensation on the off chance of some final, aghast fact. This, he keeps saying, in profusion and splendour, this is the heart of the matter and unarguable.

And it was at this time that I dreamed of perfect happiness.

For three weeks I had begun to notice that my dreaming took
on an ever greater reality. Perhaps it was because I saw and spoke
to no one that the dead in my dreams came to seem so real, as
if present in the room with me. *Quid non imminuit dies?* What
is not destroyed by time? I laughed in my dreams with delight.
But when I awoke I always had the uncomfortable feeling that I
should be punished for seeing my dead friends, and that I must
be treated for hallucinations eventually as if I were ill or mad.
In the dreams themselves I felt lighthearted, not least because
I was no longer preached at by hypocrites or taught by idiots.

I made a note of one dream as follows:

Find myself on a Penzance train going past muddy estuaries.
Hot summer's day. An old man in my compartment is translating
the Bible into Latin. Two Pekinese on the seat beside him are
panting, tongues like postage stamps in the fur. Saint Jerome's
lions? Someone I much want to ask a question just misses
the train at Liskeard. I look into a compartment on my way to
the buffet and see my friend the painter and gardener Patricia
Thoburn laughing uncontrollably with Edward Lear. He is passing
round his hat but she refuses to look at the label. Next to Lear is
sitting Jacob Ensor in a sprigged dress and beaked mask. I jump
out at Truro and, to my indescribable delight, I am met by my
most missed and high-spirited boating companion, Julian Bayley,
in his prime. In no time, with a soft evening breeze, we sail past
St Mawes. Before our boat rounds Nare Head I look up at the

big window of the old hotel, and there are Pat Thoburn, Saint Jerome, Edward Lear and Jacob Ensor again, watching us, with an elderly waitress. We slowly approach the island, Gull Rock, which is asleep in a long twilight. In the dream I distinctly hear the runnelling of water against the hull and know that the boat is painted yellow.

In America the president, for all the world like the Mad Queen in Alice, yelled 'Inject them with disinfectant!' The old kitchen wireless, my only contact with the outside world, told me this. Each evening I learned from it the statistics of the worldwide dead and heard new horrors.

Michelangelo's Last Five Drawings

But that is not all. Do not dare for a moment to think you can say anything correctly about Michelangelo.

Did you not see him once, just his back view, at the Quirinale, as an old man? By the cloister of San Silvestro, the whole of Rome spread out in a panorama beneath his feet? Probably he was there to meet Vittoria Colonna, the passionately spiritual and original thinker, for one of their conversations he so much values, about faith and the possibility of redemption.

Si prezzo a morte, e si lontan da Dio. Death so close and God so far away.

For even Michelangelo is old now, and wakes every morning with a shock to realize that he is nearly ninety. He who all but invented the notion of virility and the powerful forearm, the powerful thigh, has now to settle to the inordinately long task of dying. The mighty artist, who so much dislikes in his work to finish anything, must himself now finish. But do not dare to suppose that you can say anything correctly about what he has become or thinks he is. The most I can hope to do is tell you what he looks like on a particular day, and then discuss the last five drawings.

He is still a large man, who once was lean and sinewy. Round face, square forehead marked with seven parallel lines on the brow. A broken nose from a fight in adolescence. Large ears, thin lips, short grizzled hair. Forked grey beard, not very thick, on a strong, square jaw. He looks at you out of rather small eyes, the colour, Vasari says, of horn flecked with bluish and yellow sparks. He retains his Tuscan accent. He is often ill. Finds it hard to urinate. Has gravel in the kidneys, blood in the urine. May have to ease himself with a rod or tube. Is often in pain.

And this after a life of bodies, drawing bodies more rounded, mightier, more beautiful, more youthful, wider of rib and of a musculature more massy, with attachments suggesting force, than those seen in 5th-century BC Greece and never since. But nothing comes crashing down. It would if the drawings were *just* of bodies but they are never only that. They are drawings of ideas. He has made ideas' chief province the incomparable human form. All his life, thoughts and emotions have occurred to him in no other way than in the shape of the human body, his continual subject. Have you noticed how often the idea is bound or shackled? How often the centre or essence struggles to escape the prison of its line? How many of those perfect proportions, turning and stretching, are doing their utmost to get free? The efforts of the soul to free itself from matter.

Well, the sun-awnings shade the marble studiolo in which he draws, exactly as he has drawn every day on principle all his life, and it hurts now even to pick up the chalk. And instead of the sensual he turns to his new preoccupation, which is death and the astounding topic of the human soul.

Michelangelo, who, ever since he was young, has been the victim of loneliness and depression, has a great deal to say about death. I mean in his conversation and letters as much as in the work. Here are some of his remarks:

I am so old that often death tugs at my cloak for me to go with him.
I am not only old but almost one of the number of the dead.
You will say rightly that I am old and distracted, but I assure you that only distractions prevent one from being beside oneself with grief.
All my friends are dead.

Death is in many of the sonnets too. When he sent Rime 66 to Vasari in 1554 he wrote a covering note: 'You will surely say I am old and crazy to want to produce sonnets, but since many say I am in my second childhood I wanted to act the part.'

He says many times that he feels weighted down by years and filled with sin.

So the obsession with death very soon becomes an obsession with forgiveness and the possibility of redemption. He begins to ask how so old a man can be saved from the tyranny of the senses, how so old and sinful a man may find salvation. In a passionate way he begins to speak of faith, which he calls the gift of gifts. A simple faith in God seems to him the only chance of redemption and, through purification, of ultimate salvation.

I said at the beginning in no uncertain terms that I thought it a bad idea to analyse his thought, but an old man's memory often elides past and present, goes back and forth, and it may be interesting to mention the following:

He still knows much of Dante by heart. He can recall the sound of Savonarola's voice. In the winter he has taken to wearing heavy leggings which he keeps on for so long that, when he finally takes them off, much skin comes off with them. There was a time in August 1506 when he was trapped in Bologna by the plague. It was hotter there than he believed it could be anywhere on earth and it only rained once in eighteen months. It was Ghirlandaio who taught him to draw form by using crosshatching. His nephew, Lionardo, sent him a present once of eighty-six pears, of which Michelangelo passed thirty-three to the Pope, who seemed pleased with them. He wrote to his brother: 'I live here in Florence in great toil and great weariness of body and have no friends of any kind and don't want any, and haven't time to eat what I need.' He uses a toothed *gradina*, not a flat chisel. His mother died when he was six. Sometimes a cheerful dinner and good conversation can alleviate what seems to him not just melancholy but madness. It saddens him that all his life the workmen, his assistants, have found him strange or obsessed. He has argued with them.

But it is much too late for any of this now because his topic is all the gigantic moral and intellectual questions, which seem pointless abstractions to Leonardo but which, to Michelangelo, are all that matter: good and evil, suffering, unity with God. Such mystical devotion will not be explained.

The old impatience with completion is becoming something lovely and peculiar in itself. The Rondanini *Pietà*, begun ten years ago, he has returned to with a vengeance. He has destroyed much of it, including the head of Christ, and is every day coaxing the rest into a whole series of tender and poignant new and simultaneous possibilities. Think how different it is to that first *Pietà*, in St Peter's, done when he was not yet twenty-five. A man lying in the lap of the virgin. Both of them young, both complete, both perfect, beautiful and harmonious, and not a mark of suffering on Christ's body. Compared to that, the Rondanini carving is a wreck. In it all rules of anatomy are abandoned in the search for emotional intensity. And in it incompleteness has been found out and deliberately imposed. As an approach to the spirit, incompleteness has itself become a human value.

Let me know mine end and the number of my days. Very soon it will be February 8th, 1564. Do not attempt to guess what is running through Michelangelo's mind in these last five drawings.

All are of the crucifixion. Four include Mary and Saint John. Each drawing is blotched and marked, full of revisions, alterations, corrections, and is patently incomplete. In two the vertical of the cross has been changed using a ruler, apparently at a late stage, to a slight tilt, the better to express the dead weight of the body. For in these drawings Christ is dead. In two of the drawings his head lolls to the left and the legs are redrawn twice across the first state-ment to reposition them, building up the muscle and then taking it away. The characteristic of all five is that the bodies are narrowed by repeated reductions of the form, as if the surrounding space encroaches on them. Their horizon is chipped away by chalk marks but somehow this adds to their sculptural bulk. Mary and Saint John are in despairing attitudes. In one, Mary holds her head with both hands. In two others the distraught figures approach the body of Christ but cannot touch it. Their feet heavily grip the ground and their clothes are either absent or so rudimentary as to accentuate their nudity by wrapping round it. The body of Christ himself is beautiful beyond belief, full of hollows, the agonized muscles of the chest and stretched stomach, which are at the centre of each drawing, conveyed miraculously by a sort of smoke of changing indications within the form.

Do not say: This is drawing by an old man's shaky hand. For it is drawing by one of the greatest sensibilities there has ever been, at its wits' end.

Sculptors' Drawings

Have you been fortunate enough to talk to sculptors about drawing?

Gaudier-Brzeska, always broke, thought he had won some sort of lottery. This was in the leaking shed he used as a studio at the bottom of the Fulham Road, London, in 1913. My old friend the sculptor Leon Underwood was there. They wanted to buy a bottle with which to celebrate but could not afford one. There was torrential rain. The business of buckets. So instead they talked about life drawing and could not agree. Gaudier, like Rodin, wanted to let the model move about and tried to draw an outline without looking overmuch at the page. Whereas Underwood had hit on a system of first drawing *on* the model, putting lines round his or her arms or stomach with lipstick to indicate the section and then drawing not the horizon but the form.

But all this is like coming home with yesterday's newspaper and reading it tomorrow. Michelangelo worked at the very extremity of whatever might just conceivably be possible.

Now the delicate abundance of garden and landscape began its reckless second stanza, as though snowdrops and cowslips were no longer enough.

Orchard grass was full of dog violets, speedwell, bugle. Apple blossom, brightly lit against deep shadow, fresh pink, white, carmine, each variety with a scent of its own and heavy with honey bees and full-sacked bumble bees. In the woods was the garlic smell of sappy ransoms, their white stars among the grey-pink clumps of red campion. There was may blossom, bird-cherry. White and purple lilac opened in great profusion, parrot tulips and carpets of yellow and scarlet wallflowers warmed by the sun.

The avenue of crabapple trees was in blossom, the chestnuts decorated loftily with green-white candles, the row of oaks round-shouldered with fresh foliage. Beneath them, extensive seas of ultramarine bluebells, banks of milkmaids, ditches of cow parsley. Anchusa. Stitchwort. Forget-me-nots. The pencilled faces of dianthus. True geraniums, a fine ecclesiastical purple. Erigeron. Lily of the valley.

Surrounded by death, the beehives were busy. The evenings smelled of nutmeg and custard which was honeysuckle. At night a colossal canopy of clear constellations was bright in pure air. The slender sickle of the new moon and its neighbour Venus were of astounding brilliance and very near. May God receive my soul.

At first light, no other sound but birdsong, the cuckoo calling and the hollow drumming of green woodpeckers from near and very far, and nightingales singing all day long.

Rembrandt and Suffering

It may just be possible to talk about painting in relation to suffering.

Then the bad weather comes much later, and stays for longer, and there is little enough to eat except bread and pickled herrings. It is January 1663, on the west side of Amsterdam where the wooden rope walk is separated by a ditch from the city bulwark.

There are the last high houses of the Lijnbaansgracht where it crosses the Rozengracht, and there is the long roof of the plague-house. Beyond, the wide views over flat country, fens and reeds, a barn, a tower on the horizon. A derelict tower? A solid, immobile sky at the best of times and, at the worst, the ubiquitous sickly fog. No one about. The farms dormant. The same if you take the track by the river Amstel out towards the tongue of land called the Omval, where the inn Het Molentje stands with its jetty, moored barges and row of masts. Further off, the empty threshing floors and farmsteads, mills and the occasional thatched cottage with its wooden walls near a clump in the polderland, an apparently endless plain. In the other direction the distant silhouette of Schellingwoude village and the Ransdorp tower, the track disappearing towards the horizon. The fields fallow, not even a rowing boat moving where the Amstel and Ringvaart make a sharp bend around the Diemermeer with a group of houses and a mill. A landscape drawn with a reed pen. Is that a horse towing a barge, the barge itself out of view beyond the bank? Does life have no meaning except what you bring to it?

Because this is not intended as straightforward art history but as something half understood, I am going to tell you a short story about three women. The first is Saskia van Ulenborch (or van Uylenburgh) who came as a young girl to her cousin's house in Amsterdam and was married to Rembrandt in 1633. At the time, he had countless portrait commissions and felt himself to be relatively rich. She was cheerful and high-spirited and he could not stop drawing her. He drew her as though he could not take his eyes off her: in bed, with flowers, without flowers, dressed up, dressed down, serious or smiling and, quite soon, pregnant. Then he drew her with their baby, whose name was Rumbartus. Rembrandt, the son of a miller, had the pleasure, through Saskia's family, of introductions to interesting and distinguished people, several of whom became sitters as well as friends. She brought with her some of her father's money. See the superb etching of them sitting together, Rembrandt with his hat with a feather, Saskia watching him draw. Rembrandt described them at the time as 'abundantly blessed with riches'. They look almost opulent, and Rembrandt took many pupils.

When you get married you sometimes walk past graves. There is an etching by Rembrandt of a bride and groom passing a grave out of which rises the figure of Death. You do not have to listen very hard now to hear the bell of the Oude Kerk strike once to signal the beginning of Rembrandt and Saskia's misery. Little Rumbartus died at two months old. After him came two daughters, both called Cornelia, who lived for three weeks and two. And then, on the birth of their son Titus, Saskia began to feel ill. You watch with horror in the drawings as her plump cheeks become hollow and sickness makes her previously cheerful expression unrecognizable. So these are a different kind of bed drawings, sickbed drawings, and eight years almost to the day since she and Rembrandt were married she died. She was twenty-nine. What had begun as an idyll was over all too soon.

Now, very briefly, the second woman. It is distressing to think of her. It is possible only to see her back view in one of Rembrandt's drawings of her. She does not turn her head. Her name was Geertje Dircx and she came to Rembrandt's household as nurse to Titus, who was a year old when his mother died. Geertje Dircx was a trumpeter's widow from a village in north Holland. An acquaintance described her as a little farm woman, and plump. She wore the local costume of Waterland with what looks like rabbit fur on her bodice. At first it went well for her. When she found herself supplanted in Rembrandt's affections by Hendrickje Stoffels in 1649 she was at first disbelieving, then so angry and hurt that she took him to court pleading breach of promise. Rembrandt was required to pay her maintenance for life, not much, but a larger sum than he had intended to get clear of her. She began to pawn Saskia's jewelry, which Rembrandt had given her on the understanding that it would eventually pass to Titus. Rembrandt in turn brought a case against her and she was given an appallingly long sentence in a reformatory. He paid for her to be taken there and objected when, after five years, she was rescued by a friend who took her back to Waterland.

Third, there is Hendrickje Stoffels, a sergeant's daughter from Bredevoort. She seems to have been an exact opposite of Saskia. She joined the household on the Breestraat and before long became Titus's fond stepmother and Rembrandt's common-law wife. She was chastised for living with him by her church, prosecuted for fornication and forbidden communion. Three months later, she had Rembrandt's baby. As he had done with Saskia, he drew her repeatedly, at her domestic work or watching peaceably out of the window. Far from the high spirits and conversation of his days with Saskia, there now seems to have been an air of quiet companionship in their home. Titus in the drawings is at his table, writing, absorbed in his schoolbooks.

On the face of it, this looks like a contented enough domestic existence, but Hendrickje Stoffels's years with Rembrandt were racked by trouble with creditors, court orders, eviction orders, unpaid bills and serious debt. The seeds of disaster had been sown in 1639 when, while awaiting some late payments for pictures, Rembrandt had borrowed a large sum of money at rates of interest he could not possibly repay in order to buy his grand house. He and Saskia had been extravagant in other ways too, unable to see, of course, that taste would change and that Rembrandt's work would to some extent go out of fashion. There were other unfortunate circumstances which compounded his trouble, not least a financial recession in Amsterdam caused by the inevitable war.

While the courts moved against him, Rembrandt got further into debt when, for four years, he refused to vacate his house. When it was finally sold it raised much less than he had paid for it, and his collection of old master pictures, drawings and superb prints fetched next to nothing. He was, in effect, bankrupt. As if this was not enough, the draconian rules of his guild, the Guild of Saint Luke, forbade him as a bankrupt from selling his own work. To circumvent this, friends helped him and Titus form a small dealer's company with Rembrandt as their employee, but he was permitted to keep little of the proceeds from any sales. They found themselves in drastically reduced circumstances. Rembrandt rented rooms in an artisan area on the western edge of Amsterdam, on the Rozengracht. To raise a small sum of money he sold Saskia's grave.

Now, as I said, it is 1663 and the plague has returned to Amsterdam. Jordaan, where Rembrandt and Hendrickje live, is a poor parish outside the Keizersgracht, Amsterdam's outermost canal, and as a result is badly affected. The plague is on its way by ship to London. The nearby plaguehouse, drawn by Rembrandt, is full. See Hendrickje at her window. She is thirty-nine. She begins to look ill. The drawings, always the drawings, show that she takes to her bed. In July 1663 she, too, dies and is buried in the Westerkerk nearby.

I have described these three women because their suffering is also Rembrandt's suffering. By 1668 his beloved Titus is dead also, and Rembrandt is left alone with his fourteen-year-old daughter.

And yet. Up until his own death in 1669, Rembrandt continues to work every day in these dreadful circumstances, and a breathtaking gentleness and sympathy arises in the last few pictures that has never been surpassed. His own suffering and that of his family enables him at last to come close in the most mysterious way to expressing the very essence of what it is to be human. He does it by painting, without inflection or much movement, pictures of devotion, sympathy, tenderness and compassion. *The Jewish Bride*

(Rijksmuseum) was painted in the year Titus died. Out of a time of illness, worry and loss comes the indescribable beauty of those hands, one upon another on the breast, the astonishing passage of red material and, in the faces, one of the most marvellous realizations ever made of physical and spiritual love.

No artist could have equipped himself better to achieve this. There always had to be something more than appearances. You can detect it even in the very early drawings he made of his old blind father and determined mother, in the smudges and blots. Unusually in Leiden, he took to drawing in the street when he was a student. At first, like Federico Fellini, he delighted in the oddness of bodies and faces, not much in their beauty. They were to be invaluable to him in crowd scenes in his religious paintings. Dutch beggars and old people dressed up at the foot of the cross. He practised drawing expressions by pulling faces in the mirror, pretending surprise or rage. And, when he moved to Amsterdam and began to prosper, he was forever in the street again, drawing rapidly with a quill pen: the woman frying pancakes on the corner, and the beggars, of whom there was no shortage as disabled and destitute men returned from the wars. He was often in the auction room, bidding for costumes, armour and hats in which to dress them.

But then something comes over him: you can see that a change takes place, from almost exactly the month that Rumbartus dies. In the drawings, Rembrandt begins to look increasingly at family groups, at mothers and children in a domestic setting, at babies, a child taking its first steps to outstretched arms. Small moments to do with animals or chores like winding cotton, or looking out of the window; acts of no consequence. But there always has to be something more than appearances.

In the commissioned portraits and in the relatively intractable medium of etching, does not this oddly indefinable quality begin to become discernible too? The portraits must show the demeanour of the sitter as well as their facial expression and social status, and the objects in their rooms. But now there is something more. What seems to interest Rembrandt is something that lies behind, the part he cannot see. His way with light, his smudging and erasing, the awkward hesitations and rapid touches, the unorthodox way in which he rubs ink off the etching plate with the side of his hand. All this begins to hint at the person within, the inner life of the sitter, the shadowy character trapped somewhere out of sight. As time goes on and his life begins to unravel, the inner life becomes all that interests him. Increasingly, however desperately he needs the money, he begins to paint uncommissioned pictures. Even *Bathsheba at her Bath* (1654, Louvre), as resounding and magnificent a statement of the vulnerable human body as has ever been painted, seems not to have been done for money. Nor the *Woman Bathing in a Stream* (1654, National Gallery, London), which, to us, seems to embody the whole world of painting and feeling; let alone the carcass of a slaughtered ox (1655, Louvre).

What is it? What is it? He asks the same question all his life as he peers into his own face. The least self-pitying of documents, those self-portraits, more than fifty of them. No sympathy here for a man who showed himself once prosperous and then, breaking off sometimes with a rueful smile or a grimace, or to dress up as one person or another, becoming first sad, then despairing, then accepting, then simply an unprepossessing, prematurely aged mortal. As a combined portrait of what it is to be human, the part that does not show, they are beautiful beyond compare.

When I was in my late teens I was fortunate enough to see Rembrandt's 1657 self-portrait (National Gallery of Scotland) almost every day for two years. So obsessed did I become with the picture as pure painting that what I thought I saw was this: a face made up of broad statements rubbed, wiped and scratched by every kind of inspired revision in the way of drawing. An accumulation of impulses, very often set down quite fast and partly eliminated. It worked because of its apparent speed of execution and because the process itself remained visible, deliberately left in sight as if to excite the viewer's imagination. Its crusts and glazes, dabs, wounds, twists and turns of the brush, accidents, corrections, thoughts and afterthoughts all looked as if they were still wet. A drawing and profound re-drawing in oil paint, left off, abandoned at a beautiful stage rather than completed. It seemed to me that in the pressure of the skull beneath the skin, the awkward softness of the nose, were set up, in the full knowledge of anatomy, technique and the process of getting older, and that this was somehow done all in one, summed up and expressed undeniably and in confidence at one blow and as a single statement. And I wished that all painting could be like this.

Only now, much later, do I think to ask what suffering lies behind that glance, and realize that the picture is of something out of sight.

After this there came a celebration of white. May trees, and the double may, flowered in great profusion, lit by bright sunlight. Chestnut trees carried ever broader towers of white bloom. The white of chequer trees began. Cow parsley, Queen Anne's lace, grew tall and flowered white with great exuberance in fields and ditches. And, above white plants, the gigantic rounded heads and full sails of sun-bright cumulus swelled up as white as laundry.

The kitchen radio informed me that Iranian aircraft had infected people in the Middle East by flying illicitly in defiance of government bans. In the Bay of Bengal there were boats drifting full of dead refugees who had tried to escape the plague, not been allowed to land, and starved to death. In Britain, hospitals in need of beds began moving untested residents into care homes, sending the infection with them. In New York, an island in the East River was dug up for mass graves, but trucks full of dead in the city remained in the street for weeks because no one dared drive them away.

Frans Hals's Last Painting

Laughter. It was evidently no great hardship to be painted by Frans Hals in the 1620s and '30s. More than half of his sitters are laughing. Vincent van Gogh, an enthusiastic admirer of Hals, wrote that there's 'nothing to be said against painting *people* [. . .] The question is simply whether one takes the soul or the clothes as one's starting-point' – and 'I have to practise, though, because it certainly comes down to dexterity – they don't have much time or patience.'[1]

Hals was a fast painter. Van Gogh again: 'The work doesn't have to be any the worse if it's put down virtually in one go, and one has to be able to work even when the model doesn't sit stock still.' And then Van Gogh describes, apropos wanting to show *real* expressions, how he had been trying to paint a lively and animated girl from a brothel who said to him: 'Pour moi, le champagne ne m'engaye pas. Il me rend tout triste' (Champagne doesn't cheer me up. It makes me very sad). Then, he says, he understood, 'and tried to get something voluptuous and sad at the same time'.[2]

The expression caught in movement and painted with energy. What a mystery life is. The durable within the transitory. 'I'm working with a will,' Van Gogh says when looking at Hals, 'but one has to work all the same with aplomb and with enthusiasm.'[3] He must work more vigorously still. Hals found that, at the outset, what was most revealing for him was the smile, suppressed amusement, the laugh, even the horse's laugh. Wet lips. Wet teeth. Eyes shining with tears of laughter. 'Flemish sailors, Antwerp through and through, standing eating mussels and drinking beer, and

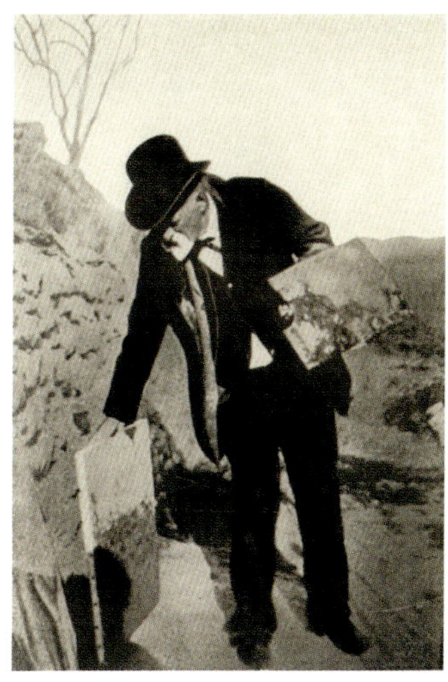

1 Paul Cézanne working on a view of Mont Sainte-Victoire
at Les Lauves, 1906.

2 Paul Cézanne, *The Cathedral at Aix-en-Provence from Les Lauves*, 1902–6,
pencil and watercolour with gouache.

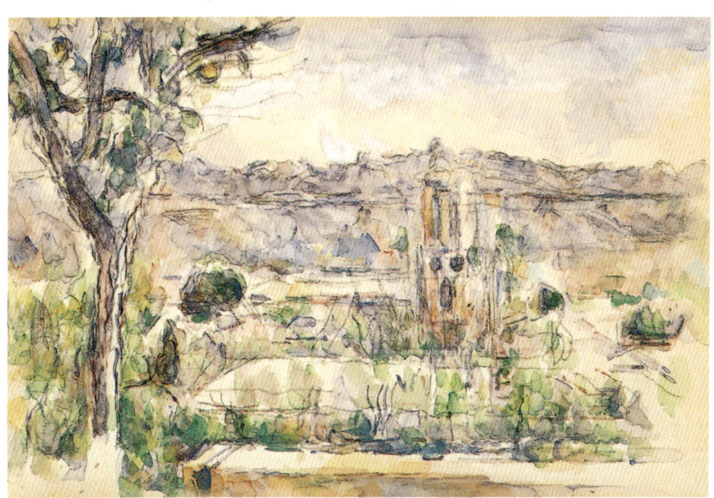

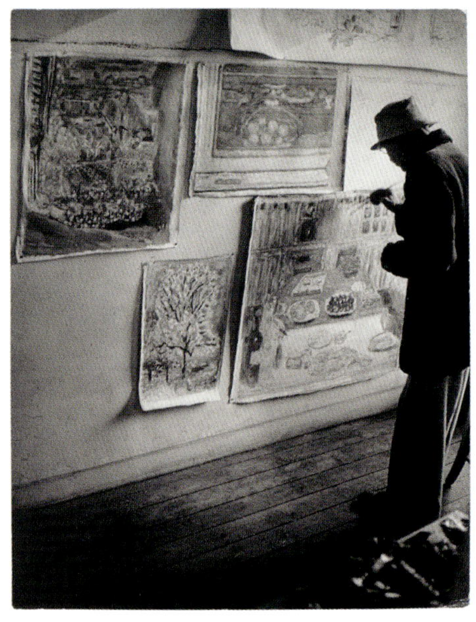

3 Pierre Bonnard painting his final four pictures, photographed by Brassaï. Le Cannet, 1946.

4 Pierre Bonnard, *La Salle à Manger*, 1942–46, oil on canvas.

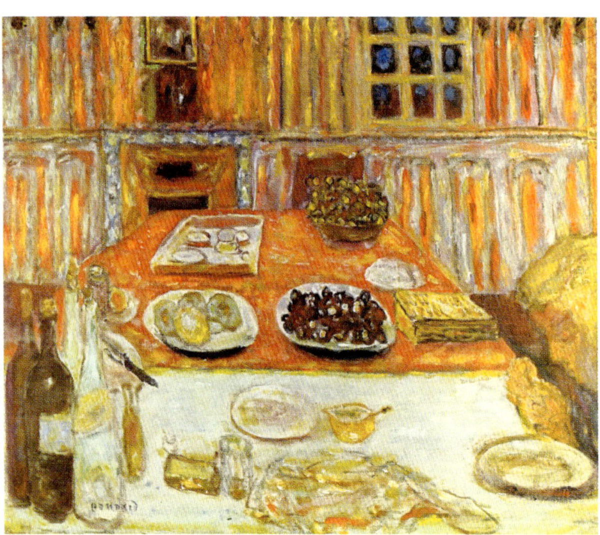

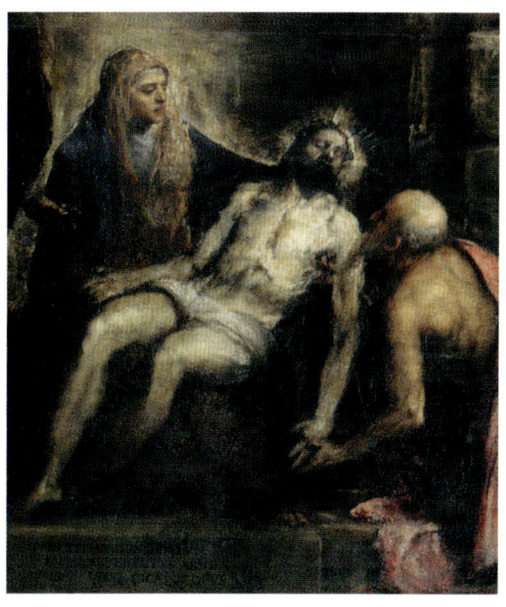

5 Titian, *Pietà* (detail), 1575–76, oil on canvas.

6 Michelangelo, *The Crucifixion with the Virgin and St John*, 1550–60, drawing.

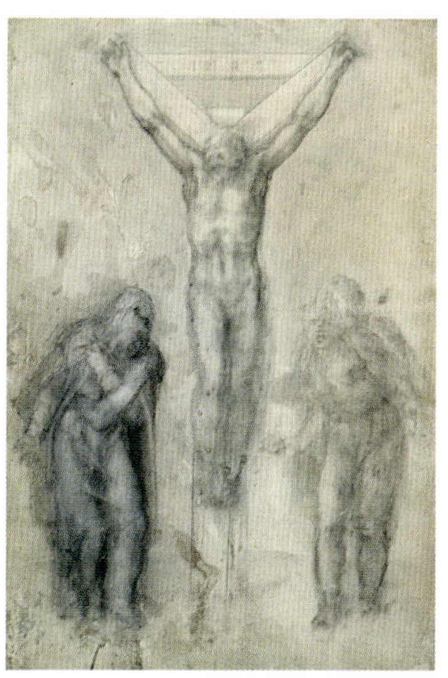

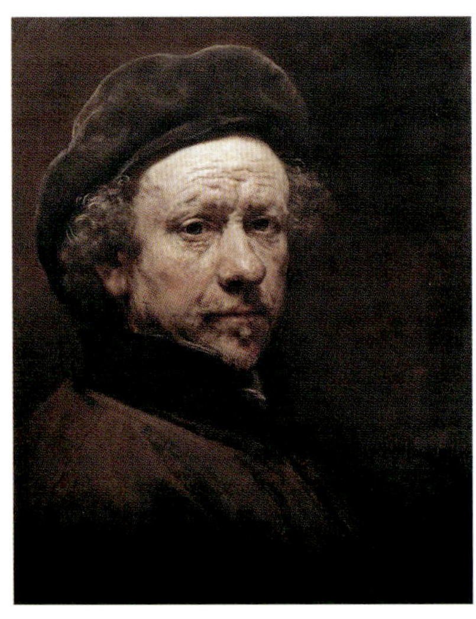

7 Rembrandt van Rijn, *Self Portrait*, 1655, oil on canvas.

8 Rembrandt van Rijn, *The Jewish Bride*, c. 1665–69, oil on canvas.

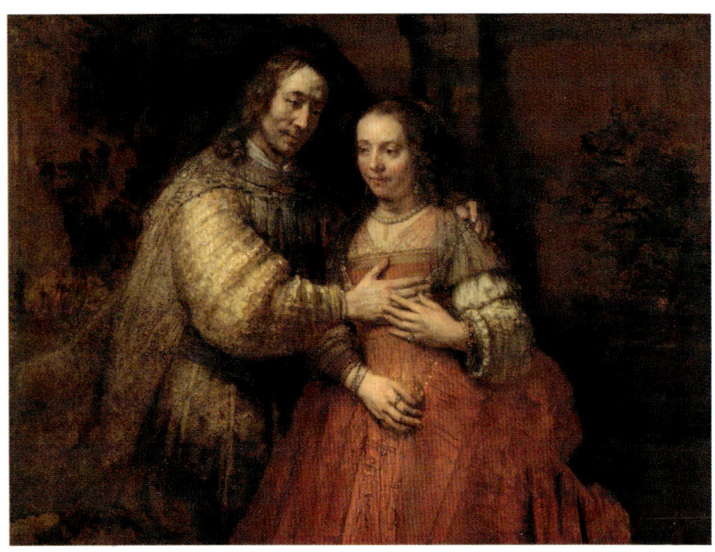

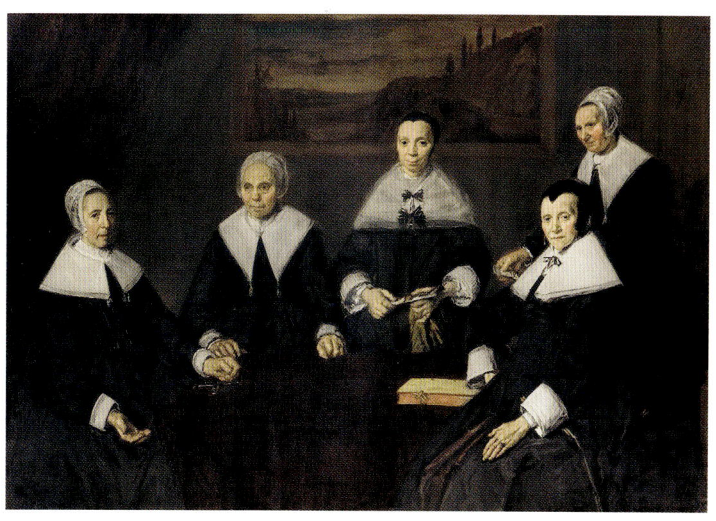

9 Frans Hals, *Lady Regentesses of the Old Men's Almshouse, Haarlem, c.* 1664, oil on canvas.

10 Camille Pissarro, *L'Église Saint-Jacques à Dieppe*, 1901, oil on canvas.

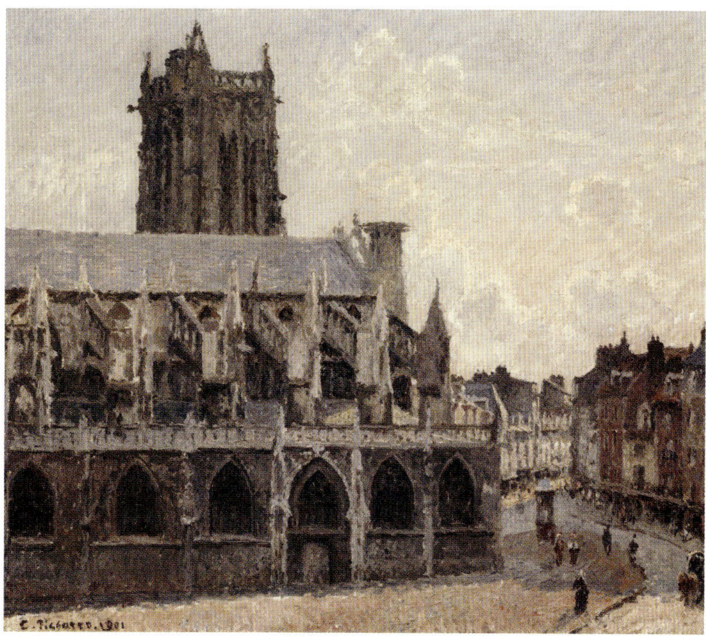

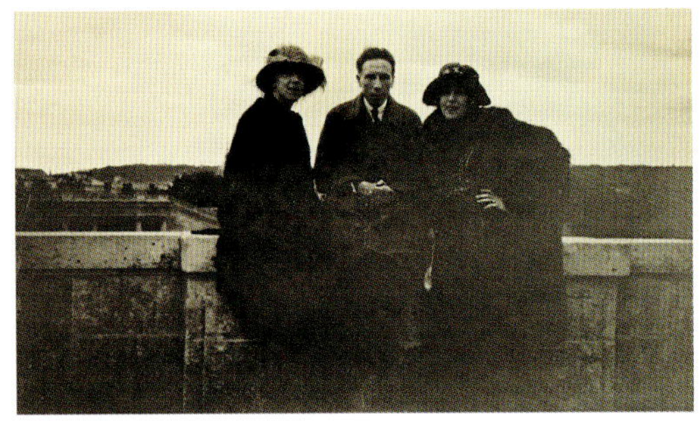

11 Gwen John (left) with Henri-Pierre Roché and Jeanne Robert Foster, 1923.

12 Gwen John, *Figures in Church*, date unknown, pencil and watercolour.

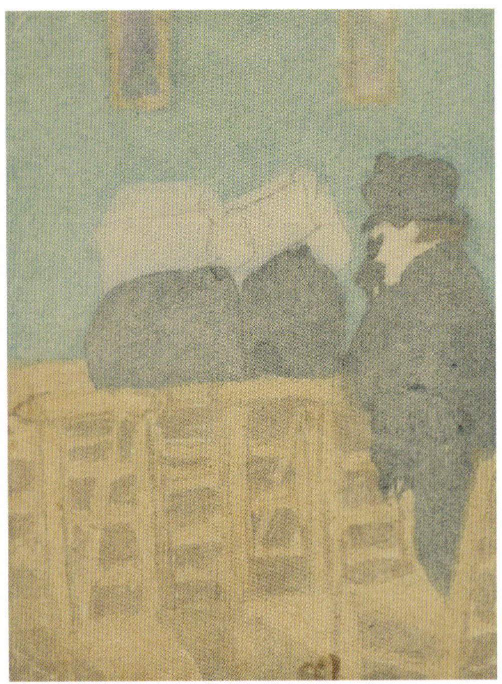

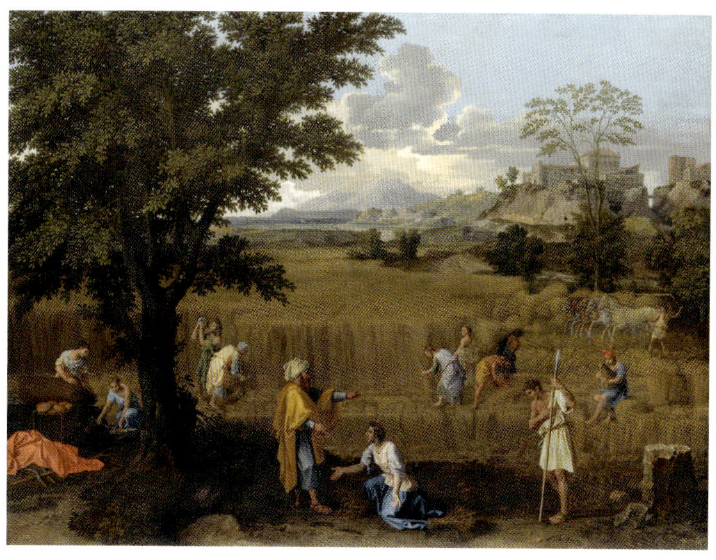

13 Nicolas Poussin, *Summer, or Ruth and Boaz*, 1660–64, oil on canvas.

14 Claude Lorrain, *Landscape with Ascanius shooting the Stag of Sylvia*, 1681–82, oil on canvas.

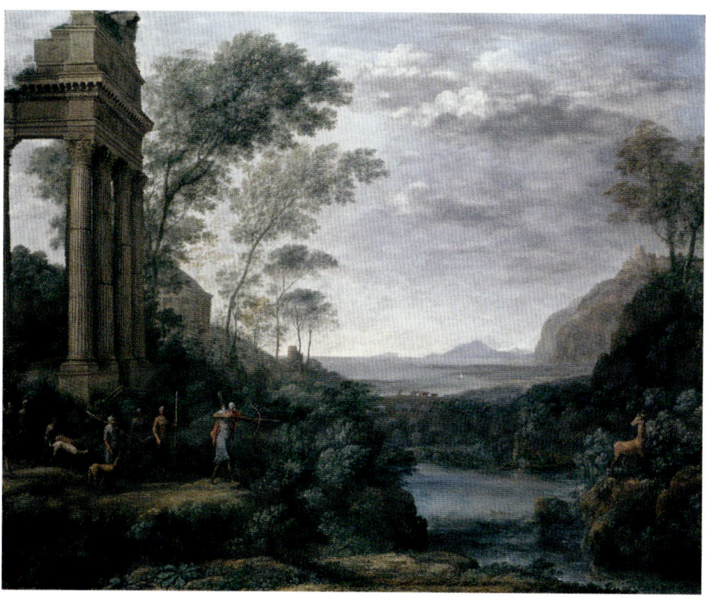

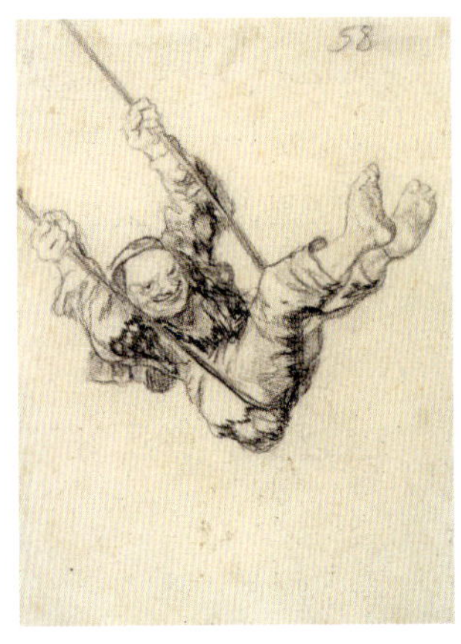

15 Francisco Goya, *Old Man on a Swing*,
1823–28, crayon on paper.

16 Diego Velázquez, *Las Meninas*, 1656, oil on canvas.

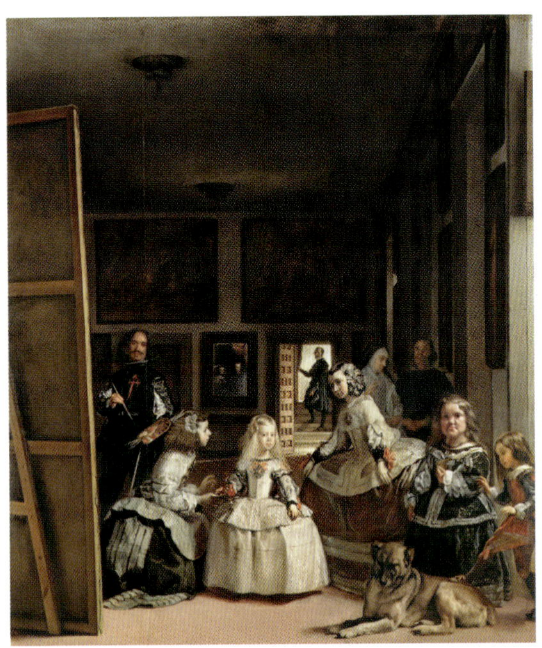

making a great deal of noise and commotion.'[4] Tumult. So the basis of sound poetry is fact. Faces are damaged by smallpox, are the colour of boiled shrimps, and hair is like pigs' bristles, but, in the lively expression, character is laid bare.

The exaggerated reaction that is a parody of the true response? Social pieties affronted? Laughter because of grotesque events? Acting by halfwits or people adopting a comic send-up of vice or virtue? Vulgarity. Such vigour suggests the feeling narrative of being human. Brewers, drinkers, boys playing the goat (Hals had eight children), actors, soldiers. Did he tell the same good joke to all of them?

And some there are who never smile. Preachers. Lawyers. Bankers. Theologians, for whom life is no laughing matter. Besides which, Hals, who had a very long career, eventually grew older. He dropped the timbre and register of the pictures several octaves. They entered a more serious room. Sometimes they were grey, or even brown. That is not in any way to suggest that the energy or vitality of his method diminished. The brushing was as fast as before, if not faster. He seemed never to make preparatory drawings but quickly found out the form and expression on the canvas with breathtaking ingenuity. Instead of the twitch of the smile, the twitch of the brush, which as quickly suggested a shadowed eye or the pulse in a temple as the crushed and faded texture of a gigantic collar or discoloured moustache. Hals's increasing ability to bring this off was admired by Courbet, Manet and Whistler, all of whom, like Van Gogh, thought it worth the trouble to go to Haarlem to see the pictures at first hand and be astonished by them.

For fifty years I have spent time each winter peering into the face of Willem Adriaan Jonkheer van Hoorn. He was seventy-eight when he sat for Hals in Leiden in 1650. The painter was approaching seventy. The picture hangs in a room with plenty of books in it and a good fire. Outside the window a stretch of water and no shortage of rhododendrons. Usually, gritty snow is falling. I was young when I first saw it. I aged while sitter and painter remained the same, and now I am as old as they are. But in this contraption for catching the human spirit is all the old man's egotism, appetite and awkward movement, and the thrilling brushwork newly catches each tone and texture and hint of meaning as if, each time I see it, I had never seen the picture in my life before. A series of apparently cursory marks, no sooner seen than realized.

But now the point of this short essay: the last pictures of all. Consider what Haarlem was like in the 1650s and '60s. For the most part, prosperous, self-confident, religiously tolerant and certainly overpopulated, with a newly developed civic sense. When there were lapses in its economic prosperity there was no shortage of people with sufficient wealth and free time to look after the poor, the orphanage, the hospitals, the leper pesthouse, the workhouse and almshouses. The guilds, too, helped their less fortunate members. In other words, there were charitable institutions which needed to be soberly and efficiently run and there had grown up a morally responsible culture of committee people to do this. It was a group of such people – the managers of the Old Men's Almshouse – who turned to Hals when he was eighty-three and less fashionable, perhaps even cheaper than some of the other portrait painters in Haarlem, and commissioned him to paint their regents and regentesses.

Hals had some experience of institutions like these. His daughter Sara had been admitted to care when pregnant after trouble with illegitimate babies by several men, and his feeble-minded son had entered the workhouse on poor relief and had his keep provided for five years by the St Elizabeth's hospital. Hals himself had recently asked for and received financial support from the burgomasters because he was unable to pay his bills. He was in debt to his baker and several other tradesmen as well as to the man who supplied his canvases. Also, in the winter he was receiving an allowance of free peat. Hals said he had often got into debt while trying to support his large family, 'keeping an eye on my people'; but the fact is that the city's most distinguished old painter had fallen on hard times. So when he embarked on these pictures shortly before his death there remained nothing of the roistering intertwined compositions of his earlier commissions, the laughing militia subjects, nor their exuberant colour. Just their low viewpoint. Examine, then, from about table height, the regentesses.

Now we are in the subdued realm of moral rectitude. The figures are set out in a row across the canvas. Three of them look the painter in the eye. Two seem unable to do so. Death is present. Death is all around.

It is in their faces. These people fear the church, take their position with the utmost seriousness and are severe in the rectitude of their service to society. The woman third from the right, with the inexpressibly beautiful brushing by Hals of her face and collar, is both almost girlish and not as young as she was, one of the most touching demeanours he ever painted. The older woman beside her, with slightly clenched hands, looks sideways, for all the world as if you just saw her shift her glance. And the regentess on the right, with the alarmingly high colour on her cheeks and the flat hand made of half a dozen swift marks, does she not epitomize all moral seriousness and moral servitude? Here are high-mindedness, piety, the ideals of sublimation and self-repression, the devout, the orthodox, and belief in an unquestionable social benefit to society. For these women, God exists and life has meaning in good works and in the advance of humanity. It is an idea which insists cantankerously on its own boundaries.

There is as much psychology and as much life in this simply ordered row of human beings as you could ever hope to see. In them, I think, Hals identifies his own ageing. There is an underlying sadness, a resolution and a summing up. At the last moment, he paints his truest and most beautiful picture.

Then came the time of buttercups. Fields, jugs, jars and buckets full of buttercups. The waxiness of their petals on sunny evenings. A tide, a reverie of childhood buttercups.

The elder with its winey breath and creamy umbrels. Dog roses, their delicate petals shaded china-pink at the edges. And the climbing honeysuckle. Often honeysuckle, dog roses and elder climbed through each other. The whitethroat sang loudly in the blackthorn, and, if you walked in the buttercups so that your shoes turned yellow, you saw that among the stems were red clover and the tiny sparks of grass vetchling.

Meanwhile, the mad president of Brazil made his people continue to work so that large numbers of them were infected and died. The dictator in Nicaragua denied the plague existed and had the dead quickly taken away for 'express burials'. Shulan, a city of 700,000 in north-east China, was entirely sealed off from the surrounding countryside.

Many buildings in Amsterdam were found to be empty, the inhabitants having either died or fled some weeks before.

Camille Pissarro at a Window

The somewhat battered grey shutters on the fourth floor of the Hôtel du Commerce, in old Dieppe, have been open each afternoon. If you cross the Place Nationale, stand with your back to the north door of Saint-Jacques and look up to your left on this particular afternoon, July 26th, 1901, you can make out the olive face and white beard of Camille Pissarro at his window, with a crumpled hat on, hoping it will rain. He has just written to his son, Lucien. 'I have already started several canvases of the effects of rain. I dared begin because, after such tropical heat, I thought it could not fail to rain.' But no. It continues hot. A perfect Impressionist day. Small, high clouds in a cornflower-blue sky. Swifts squeaking. A priest in a black robe on his way to the boulangerie. Five women have arranged kitchen chairs on the pavé outside the violin shop on the corner, closed, and are exchanging sharp Norman gossip. A pigeon flies up to meet its shadow on the tower. An early drunk comes out of a café and doffs his beret in the direction of Duquesne. There is conversation about honey, preserves, rabbits, radishes. The sounds of knives and forks in a house blind with creeper. Flat, cracked clatter of the church clock of Saint-Rémy. In fact, another archetypal Dieppe July day. Pissarro's eye bothers him. It has bothered him since 1884. Trouble with a lachrymal duct. He will need to have it cauterized.

There are countless other windows in mansard roofs which you can look up at at various times and see Pissarro and his easel. One is overlooking the jetty at Le Havre (August 1903) and a particularly good one is high up in the Hôtel du Quai Voltaire, in Paris, with its grey view of the Seine (March 1903). I have also seen him at a window in the Hôtel du Louvre, and on the second floor of a house at the corner of the Pont Neuf and the Quai.

At Dieppe he has the excellent and very beautiful problem of the great church of Saint-Jacques. It is a problem because the building's originally rather white stone is now largely black and does not easily register the shadow of architectural detail. The interior is like a steel engraving and in bad repair. Very high up in the nave, someone is practising the organ. It is a brown organ, but thunderous, and the organist seems a tiny figure on a ledge. On the south side of the building, in the angle of the transept, no light penetrates because of the houses nearby, and there is a market cross long colonized by a widow and the many cats she feeds there. And to the east, around the apse, there is a sensationally grotesque assortment of very black gargoyles, on one of which remains the expressive black hand of a snapped-off devil.

'*Travaille encore un peu avant le mourir.*' Do a bit more work before dying. Pissarro, whose greatness consists in his humility, is soon absorbed in taking one of his Saint-Jacques pictures forward. He is seventy-one, the son of a Martinique shopkeeper and a Creole mother, always travelling, it seems to him, and never arriving. He seldom sells a picture. His absolute devotion to his method has kept his family poor. Madame Pissarro is worn out with it. These days he leaves her behind at Eragny, to an amiable peasant existence in the old farmhouse on the straight village street, with washing and children, but he is afraid she is sometimes bitter. Monet, after all, is now a success. But when there is talk of this, and mention of who has won prizes and who has won medals, and who has had successful exhibitions at the Galerie Durand-Ruel, Pissarro in his good-natured way always smiles and says '*Il n'y a que la peinture qui compte.*' It is only the painting which matters.

'To do a little more work before dying.' In fact he does a very great deal more work. As he says, he never lets go. He works every day except when the affliction of the eye prevents him. It is partly the urgent need for money that drives him but it is also something much greater. Other artists know this and regard him with amazement and respect. He needs to satisfy himself that in the end his method can be brought to some higher conclusion. With the utmost care he must somehow step from experience to experience without losing the thread of his first idea.

Old Zoë, the concierge, shouts up at him something about hare but he is too preoccupied to reply. Such exactness of observation puts him in a trance. There is a self-portrait he painted almost thirty years ago with exactly the same expression on his face that he wears now. It was the time that he and Cézanne were working, easel to easel, in the street at Pontoise and Auvers. The paint is fresh, the scribbled drawing a system of greys, browns and ochres against a cream and blue background. In those days he was closer to Corot. Luminous shadow over the brown eyes, the light softly touching the side of his head and getting in among the patriarchal beard. He may be squarer and more tired now but his appearance and vitality remain unimpaired.

No hurry ever comes over him. He works steadily away with a sense of the amplitude of time. Each picture is one step in a life-long journey against the grain of time. The pictures are objects grown old with gentle use, like pipes or hats. Painting them, he is complete in the present, whole, open, consistent, permanent. He knows very well that the act of painting is valuable in itself. It is a mistake to think that you can discuss the heart of things without first discussing their surface. Some repetition is inevitable. Now that he possesses very much more past than future, memory has become a function of awareness. He has patiently accumulated an inner world settled into an intelligible and coherent memory. We forget even good jokes and surprises. What we remember is the profound cathartic experience that transcends individual memories. I think Pissarro has trained his mind and senses to be attentive to time, to be alert to the truths of his past so that now something very remarkable can happen, something that stands outside the mind's normal precincts.

From his window he watches Saint-Jacques repeat its black and white motif of diapered buttresses agitated by his short, clotted brushstroke, the mouldings of soot and pigeon droppings, the grey-black shuttered tower. The light has come round, making what clouds there are only just discernible against the brightness of the sky. A nun crosses the street. There are notices pasted on the kiosk about a *cirque*. Among the stucco housefronts are warmer ones of brick. The yellow gravel where the market takes place meets the grey pavé, and there is a small incident of sunlight in rue Saint-Jacques. Pissarro has painted such things with attention for forty years. Soon the final sentence of his last letter to Lucien will read: 'I see that we Impressionists are far from being understood – quite far – even by our friends.'

But now, look what happens in these black church pictures and in the big, lobster-pink canvases of Dieppe's inner harbour and quay, done from another window, where a wriggle of barely legible smoke dissipates and incidents like bollards, a winch, a shed are graffiti on the sandy paste of the ground. Something inexplicable has overcome the whole process. He has always drawn with a full heart, accumulating touches of information that contribute to the ensemble. And then, out of nowhere, this soft tormenting turns and becomes resplendent and unimpaired in its own right. With apparent ease the divided colour and vibrating light come together as one ineffably rich substance, an exhilaration of innumerable marks, a fabric close in tone and wonderfully harmonious in emphasis. From its quiet poetic state some extraordinary resolution takes place, quite naturally and apparently of its own volition. After long persistence, the solution turns out to transcend all effort and produce itself.

I continued, off and on, to work at the old figure of Time. The side of his head and one ear were badly damaged as though part of his personality had been carried away, and his long thorax, with its pleasant pattern of muscle and bone where his floating ribs should be, was wounded. A hard body, no stranger to the pleasures of lichen, damaged by time in ways unknown to a soft one. On good days, when writing had been less than usually hard and there was plenty of time, I slowly gave him back his rounded form, the swelling that begins within. His attenuated, pale shape pleased me, and the big shadows in his hollows when the sun was bright.

In time I mended his cranium.	Donatello is eighty in 1466.
And in time I mended his chest.	Donatello is so old that he has nothing to lose in his last three sculptures.
Much later I mended his pelvis.	Donatello's scandalously original and expressive distortions
I mended the fold of a drape.	are the earliest and most extreme examples of late style, and the most spiritual.
And finally I mended his shins.	Christ walked not on water but on anxiety.
But I mended not his mouth.	Because Delacroix says that he at last realized how to paint when he had neither teeth nor breath.

Gwen John and Absence

You saw her once, or perhaps several times, but did not know that it was her. She draws in that way that has its origins in her Slade training, rather quickly. '*Vite, vite, vite!*' she says to herself, drawing in pencil or occasionally in charcoal and all of a piece. You could have seen her crossing the street, perhaps on her way to buy coley for the cats. Several times you have wanted to have a word with her or wanted to see a picture, but have always just missed her. You want to ask her about her idea. Just missing her is very like not quite grasping her idea. You arranged to meet but must have somehow mistaken the time or place. Either she was not there or you were not there, or perhaps it was the wrong year.

It was in the church at Meudon, about the winter of 1919 or '20, that you saw her. Small cloche hat. Brown coat given her by Ursula Tyrwhitt. She was kneeling behind two nuns, a girl and an older woman, partly drawing them and partly praying. She drew on a scrap of paper extremely small. That was nearly twenty years ago.

Now you have taken the train from Gare Montparnasse, twelve minutes only to Meudon, a village-like suburb of Paris near the forest and the river, and found your way to rue Babie. Sometimes, partly out of necessity, she draws in a single line and extremely small. But what characterizes her drawing and everything else she does is a most beautiful seriousness, an extreme sensitivity and a slight but perceptible oddness which makes you catch your breath and remain still when you see it.

Number 8 rue Babie is a piece of waste ground surrounded by tall trees with a small shed or cabin on it and a rectangular patch with signs of a garden. She is not there. A cat on the path. It is now the middle of September, 1939. September 18th, in fact. War was declared a fortnight ago and it is getting late to ask her about her idea.

How are you to know that today she has felt the need to go to the sea?

I am not going to use her name when writing about her. She is too private for that. Literal resemblance. Natural resemblance, she wrote in one of her countless notes to herself. Method. Personal form drawn, filled in *au besoin*. Her notes are half in English and half French. I cannot describe her because my pen should not touch the page, she being more of an atmosphere or a state of mind. It is correct to say that she is deliberately solitary and prefers not to talk. She eats very little, needs very little, and being very poor does not trouble her. She wrote: What a world is open to us when our mind is in peace. A world of eternal things. What sweetness in humble, solitary work, what pleasures. Pleasures we miss when we are in *société* or agitated.

Often she has taken to including the tall ladderbacks of prayer-chairs in her church drawings. They lend a pleasing geometry. Also she colours her drawings when she gets home, using watercolour or gouache, filling in the shapes with clear washes or subdued patterns which somehow add to their unexpectedness. Her Russian neighbour once told her in no uncertain terms that it was wrong to draw in church and this disapproval saddened her. But she prays a great deal, or tries to, and drawing seems to her mind to be a kind of praying. She was received into the Catholic church not long after she came to live in Meudon in 1911. The thought of God, she jotted down in her notebook, is the answer to all our questions. If we are religious enough, we should live happily.

I am still trying to approach her idea. It must be done indirectly. Considering the difficulty she had with people and with some of her sitters, she once had a most fortuitous commission. You are only free when you have left all, she wrote. Leave everybody and let them leave you. Then only will you be without fear. She became friendly with some of the Dominican Sisters of Charity at Meudon, of the congregation known as the Présentation de la Sainte Vierge de Tours, and they asked her to paint a portrait of their founder, Marie Poussepin.

Ever since her time at the Slade she had principally painted portraits or self-portraits, because of the concentration on life-figure drawing there. Almost always she had painted friends and acquaintances, hands in laps, eyes cast down or looking absently past her. But to do that she had sometimes to talk to them, even have them to stay, with all the tiresomeness that entailed to do with food and clean sheets and the agreeing of dates, and the tedium of meeting them off the train. Now the great advantage of Marie Poussepin was that she had died in 1744. Any paintings of her would have to be based on small, black and white reproductions like prayer cards of a portrait belonging to the mother of the House of the Congregation. Mère Poussepin, a half smile on her face, posed simply in her habit and coif, did not move or talk between 1913 and 1921 while seven versions of her were painted, each more tender and beautiful than the last. Anything good, the artist wrote, must be done in austere silence. It requires a quiet mind for me to paint.

Occasionally the drawn-out business of painting 'my nun', as she called her, got on her nerves, but the task answered several of her needs beyond a sense of sanctity, not least a preference for repetition, a high key, exceedingly dry paint and a certain peculiar angularity to the pose. Something unexplained about the form. Paint as you do your drawings, she told herself. It is of consequence that she did her best to work on all the versions of Mère Poussepin simultaneously, as though they were one picture. She went on to paint other nuns. From then on her paintings and drawings were frequently in series. Sometimes there are as many as twelve versions of the little drawings made in church, as though there must be a perfect solution to the arrangement if only she could reach it. I think, she wrote once in a letter, that my vision will count because I am patient and *recueilli*, contemplative, in some degree.

But the idea. The idea. When you found her absent from her piece of waste ground in rue Babie you could have turned and walked the short distance to 29 rue Terre Neuve. This house was demolished in the 1960s. In it, on the fifth floor, were the three little rooms and *grenier*, attic, which she had long used as her writing and drawing place. There always seemed to be something the matter with the stairs. She liked a remark of Maurice Denis: 'The power to suggest connections between ideas and objects has always been the point of art.' Of these much-loved rooms, which cost almost nothing every three months when she took them in 1911, what she most appreciated and painted most often was the way in which the light came into the small bedroom that faced east, especially when the net curtain was caught back by a book. When she had first come to Paris she earned a little money by posing as an artist's model. She had drawn herself both dressed and undressed and posed her sitters sometimes for several weeks in this room. If one can do a square inch that pleases one, she wrote, one ought to be happy. There was a wicker chair, a small bookcase, two little watercolours on the wall that look as if they are of her favourite cat, named after boulevard Edgar Quinet, done when she and Dorelia McNeill lived together in Paris in 1904.

It is surely superfluous to say that today she is not at rue Terre Neuve either. But many of the notes towards her idea are. Often she has felt that there must be so much weakness in her, doing so little work and never exhibiting. Once, when she was persuaded to show with her brother, the exhibition comprised more than thirty paintings by him and two by her. He roars like a lion on her behalf, and cannot bear that water runs down her walls and that she has little to eat, but the truth is he has always inhibited her. On another occasion, when she reluctantly agreed to send in a picture to the New English Art Club in London, her painting arrived, almost to the day, six years late. She chided herself for being so slow and uncertain in her work, but she could not abide letting anything leave until she was satisfied with it. Consequently she sold very little and went to endless pains to avoid dealers and gallery owners. She felt that her one American patron, John Quinn, had little or no grasp of what she was attempting and usually felt compelled to let him down.

Starting hesitantly in 1921–23, and continuing right up to April 1938, there are the poignant notes and lists. Here are some of them.

> Faded pansies on the sands at night. [Then some numbers
>   referring to the colours and tones of sky and clouds.]
> Colour harmony: Elderberries and their yellow leaves and pink
>   campions and their *centre bleu* green leaves.[1]

Then, most mysteriously, in a list headed 'The Making of the Portrait':

1. The strange form
2. The pose and proportions
3. The atmosphere and notes
4. The finding of forms

And in another note about method of observation:

1. The strangeness
2. Colour
3. Tones
4. Personal Form[2]

Some of the little watercolours show that, as well as gardening at rue Babie, she had started to draw plants. Well, not plants exactly but curiously offset, small-scale, experimental, almost non-representational flowers, leaves or even twigs. They are of great strangeness. They are not unrelated to the semi-abstract quality that begins to come over many of the drawings of figures in church. A Palm Sunday drawing of a girl holding a leaf is more shape than content. The geometry of church furniture, a chair leg, a cupboard, the side of some box or column unexplained, begins to be as much the subject of the drawing as the part or parts of the physical presence of people themselves. Habits and coifs make abstract shapes and figures in the background, patterned or washed with colours, become unexpected passages of modest timbre and unlooked-for tone.

Now she takes this a stage further in the garden. Why, she asks herself, do I find myself moved or somehow made to wonder by something as faint as the smell of a wild flower or the undercolour of its leaf? Long ago she had learned from Whistler not to begin a painting until she had first organized with great precision its colour and gradations of tone and hue on her palette. Look always for the small and disallowed, the least and the strangest, the faintest colour and the shyest form. In the dusk, the little silhouette and the indistinct sound.

Here are some more excerpts from her beautiful and mysterious notes to herself about colour and life, which read like poems:

> Faded dewberry flowers
> blacks   flowers ground
> paynes gray   arrange raw umber
> black
> Blackberry flowers
> black flowers ground
> Vert du chrome   yellow ochre   ochre brun
>   naples yellow   ochre brun
>   lemon yellow   ochre rouge
>   black
> Faded brown pansy. Orphan in church. (quiet happiness).[3]

> My temptations –
> 1. sitting before people, listening to them in an idiotic way.
> 2. undergoing their influence – being what they expect,
>   – *demandeé*.
> 3. by fear flattering them.

4. being too much touched – valuing too much their signs of
   friendship, or rather responding too thoughtlessly.
5. thinking too often of people.[4]

(dangers)
being *amoureuse*, my painting, unkindness of people.
Impoliteness of people.

les partirs, les retours. Fatigue.
la stupidité du monde. Manqué de temps dans mes affaires.
smoky corn and wild rose.
faded roses (3 reds).

nuts and nettles
faded primroses and dandelions
milky bluets (cornflowers)
grey and yellow plaid.[5]

Her last works, probably done eight or ten years before her death,
are small pencil marks on tiny pages, small experiments of great
presence made of next to nothing. Things of consequence made
almost out of absence. The strangeness. The strangeness.

Today she has fed the cats and gone to the sea. In fact she has
gone to Dieppe on the train. She arrives but does not feel well. She
sits on a bench by the sea. She is taken to the Hôpital Normale in
rue Pasteur. She has no name or means of identification on her,
and dies anonymously.

And then it was early summer and the roses began to open. How strangely things divorce themselves from the past and move into the present. According to Aristotle, time is a dimension of motion. Because the weather was hot the roses opened in a matter of days and in this order: Gloire de Dijon, Fantin-Latour, Souvenir du Docteur Jamain, Charles de Mills, Louise Odier, Rosa Mundi, Madame Hardy, Variegata de Brabant, Madame Isaac Pereire, Gloire des Mousseux. Those were the first.

In the early morning, when light touched newly open buds, they held a fragrant shadow of indescribable delicacy. And in the late afternoon, when the sun lay luxuriantly across the configurations of their marvellous centres, they seemed to transcend time. Each day more bourbons and gallicas, more damasks and albas. Each hour the unfurling of more centifolias and old Scottish moss roses. In the rose garden they stood waist-deep in forget-me-nots, old geraniums the colour of purple robes, foxgloves and ox-eye daisies. Ethereal colour and warm scent. More than dreaming because both detailed and universal.

The kitchen radio: in Yemen there was a desperate shortage of medical oxygen and almost no food for an already starving population. In Chile many thousands were dying each day. Fragile healthcare systems in sub-Saharan Africa were becoming overwhelmed.

Claude, Poussin and Time

Now the two men go into the house in Rome and sit down together to talk. They speak in French, one haltingly and with a slight stutter, the other with a rather ponderous seriousness. It is a pleasure to both of them to meet occasionally and speak French together and in recent years it has become a habit. Agnese, Claude's daughter, who lives with him, helps him with the presents which he always brings with him.

Both men prefer to live simply. Poussin keeps no servant and his needs are minimal. All either of them really wants to do is live quietly and get on with their work. Both, though Frenchmen, have lived in Rome practically their whole lives. Claude's house in via Paolina (now via del Pabuino), near Piazza di Spagna, is only two or three streets from Poussin's and, painting being a lonely business, they much value their conversations. I say conversations but I am not sure that either listens very closely to what the other is saying. This is because, though both hold in their heads the same extraordinary landscape, they see it in totally dissimilar ways. Claude talks about paradise and Poussin does not listen. Poussin talks about paradise and Claude does not listen. And the person who sees paradise most clearly of all is not there, and is blind.

I do not know if you have ever had the experience of talking on a regular basis to an artist who believes that pictures can be worked out rationally, that the exercise of the intellect and adherence to mathematical principles can be used to arrive at a perfect composition? Listening to Poussin say this every few weeks with absolute conviction, Claude sits with a faraway look in his eyes. He is thinking of blue. Once, when he was a young man, he saw the Gulf of Naples and he has never recovered from its blue. Now it is 1662 and he is well over sixty. Still he can think of nothing but the light in his eyes and of blue.

Poussin, who is seven years older, has changed everything, partly by thinking of the world in terms of the golden mean: $\frac{1}{2}$ ($\sqrt{5} \pm 1$). But Claude is talking about Paris and about his old assistant, Desiderii, about Tassi and someone he calls Goffredo. He is not a lucid man and his memories do not arrive with any fluency but, as well as the *dolci*, he has brought with him the fat volume in which he records his recent compositions, should Poussin be interested to see them. The drawings in this, in black and brown ink on blueish paper, are so fluid and expressive, so full of incident and shadow and trees against the light, and what he refers to as *frissons* (shivers or excitable incidents) of the pen, that they effortlessly outstrip his limping French. The two men, sitting in Rome, are transported in their memories the short distance into the slumbering Campagna, to Tivoli, where they went together when young to draw and which lies only a cart ride away with its rocks and hills, pools and vegetation, Roman bridges, little towns on cliffs, flocks, acres of scantily clouded sky, and broken architecture from antiquity, all round them in the sun. And, thinking of this, they think not only of a place but a time.

By making perfect geometric constructions, Poussin believes he can not only satisfy the mind but transcend time.

Poussin. You have to envisage a man with a long, solemn face, uninterested in small talk. Deep voice. Cartesian by persuasion. Logical, rational, extremely systematic. And thorough, above all thorough. Nothing, you feel, will he leave to chance. But, with this, a certain reticence and humility, even to the extent that he turns down all honours and will do his best to eradicate any traces of himself in the way of gesture or brushstroke. In such a beautiful system there can be no room for temperament. From the paintings, his personality must be entirely absent.

They sit under the vine outside what used to be Poussin's *caprile* or goatshed. Behind it, up two Roman stone steps of gigantic size, is the small barn he uses as a studio. Many big pictures have been painted, and will be painted in future, for instance by Courbet, in small rooms. It is the time of year of wasps and flying ants. Flying ants are bad in the kitchens. As he sits talking, Poussin is frequently making a sideways flapping movement with his hand as though irritably warding off flying insects, when in fact what he is doing is warding off theories. They bother him constantly, as much from the future as from the past. The air in the goatshed is thick with them.

'You seem to think I have all the time in the world,' says Poussin. It annoys him that Claude is always late. Claude's eye continues to range over the distant panorama in his mind.

'Oh, am I late?' he asks the horizon. 'I was looking at infinity.'

'It is a strain,' Poussin goes on in his usual vein, 'the past co-existing with the present, the real with the ideal, the grand with the intimate.'

'Is it?' To Claude, forms melt and lose solidity. Even figures become unreal as they are elongated past recognition.

Poussin, who lacks human companionship, must put up with Claude's poetic dreaming occasionally and knows how to humour him.

'The drawing of yours I was telling you about,' he says. 'You did it long ago when we were in the Campagna together and you gave it to me. Two men holding an ox. An impressive pen drawing.'

'From Virgil?'

'From life. There is the eye and the mind.' Poussin brushes away a wasp. 'It is necessary to work at their mutual development, in the eye by looking at nature, in the mind by the logic of organized sensations.'[1]

Claude sighs inwardly. Not again. He noticed this morning that he has let a pot plant die for lack of water, he who will alter the whole course of English gardening in the 18th century. When it comes to watering, he lacks time.

'Painting from nature is not copying the object,' Poussin goes on. 'We don't want to copy nature. We don't want to reproduce.

We want to produce.' Another flying ant. 'We want to produce like a plant which produces fruit, and not reproduce.'[2]

He sips his wine but does not particularly favour it. It is yellow and heavy, honeyed. He gives it to Claude because it comes from the Campagna.

'Simplicity, order, equilibrium,' Poussin says. 'Formation is the result of inner necessity.' Flying ants greatly trouble him in numbers. 'Ratio-related areas of form, or proportions, have their own life. In logic we can attain a depth of concentration which leads to a state of unawareness in the artist. It can address the human spirit.'[3]

Claude shifts uneasily on his chair. The ants don't bother him. This kind of thing, the idea that the function of art is to communicate to the spirit, makes him feel tired and irritable. A wasp gets to him.

'Sometimes I think there is too much damned profundity and not enough art,' he says crossly.[4]

Poussin looks at him. Poor Claude, he thinks. He has a bun face. It is true that, when he is angry, Claude's eyes look like currants in a pastry of some sort. And he surprises Claude by agreeing with him, not at all annoyed.

'I do so agree,' he says, disarmingly. 'Painting should be distant, considered, reticent. Even remote. There is no need to over-egg.' He cannot help continuing to think of Claude's baking. He knows his first job in Paris was as a pastry cook. Does not Rossini give up writing operas in favour of cooking?

'Not so much profundity,' he says, 'as working out the geometry. Geometry attracted me from the beginning.'

Not again, thinks Claude. The golden mean.

'The whole arsenal of Euclidean geometry,' Poussin says, 'of which the golden section is one important weapon, provides me with formal logic, though it is not an end in itself. You can't paint like this while whistling, you know.'

He bites one of the baklava-like *dolci*, savours it for a minute and then says, 'Music!'

Claude partly wakes up. He has not heard this line of reasoning before. He watches an outsize wasp land unnoticed on Poussin's honey-covered hand. The wasp is Leibniz.

Poussin says, 'Music is the hidden arithmetical exercise of a mind unconscious that it is calculating.'

I shall give it a little longer, Claude thinks, before I volunteer to look at whatever he is working on. Meanwhile I shall persevere with my own idea of the sensation of depth and the effects of light and air. I will not try to explain them. I am poor anyway at explaining, and who can explain colour? Or mood, for that matter. Perhaps what I should like most to paint is mood, and that is certain to seem obnoxious, even risible as an aim, to Poussin with his geometry.

'Harmony!' Poussin says. He seems to have lapsed into exclamations of a single word.

Harmony, to me, thinks Claude, and then stops, unable to articulate what he means by harmony. It exists in his own work, he knows, but he does not cook it up. The sun itself. The sun itself is harmony.

'*L'ordre du monde!*' Poussin has risen and is repeating '*L'ordre du monde!*' It is as if he is going over in his mind some imperative, some project to which he feels committed. He is very serious. Chateaubriand, another flying ant, would say that by this time he feels the increasing isolation of age and that his hands tremble. He is sixty-eight. He has had shaky hands since he was fifty.

Fearful for his own identity, Claude feels quite suddenly that he should leave despite the two great pictures which, if he wanted to, he could see in Poussin's barn a few yards away. He does not, of course, know that he, Claude, will be seriously ill in 1663, and so although they are close physically the paintings are some distance away in time, more than three years away in fact. When he finally sees them, there will be four last pictures in total and his friend Poussin will be dead. Not knowing any of this, Claude explains that he has remembered Agnese, who is very young, has need of him in via Paolina and that he must go. It is a question of time.

When Claude recovers from his coming illness he will go on to paint the poetic Roman countryside combined with antique grandeur in an increasingly wonderful way. The characters from Ovid, Virgil and the Bible in his foregrounds will diminish, become no more than token as he looks past them or above them and raises his eyes to the view. He will continue painting until he is eighty-two. By then the incidents, the ostensible pretexts of the pictures, will be history because his subject will become the sun. The sun's infinitely subtle and beautiful transforming effect on atmosphere as Claude paints range upon range, ignoring all conventions of balanced composition, further and ever further back across the land or across areas of shallow, rippling sea to the distant blue horizon, and beyond even that to infinity. And in the process he will have painted, in an unpremeditated way, time and the harmony of man and nature. Chemistry, unintended, will do him a distant favour too. His paint, and with it his distances, will in time become an ever more lovely blue.

But now he takes up his *Liber Veritatis* of drawings and goes hurriedly away without really saying goodbye. Best not to say goodbye. Poussin thinks Agnese provided the *dolci*, but in fact Claude always likes to bake them himself and is too modest to say so.

Poussin turns, not without relief, and goes quickly up the two steps into the studio.

Involuntarily he takes a deep breath and re-enters his own world of unimpaired landscape. It is a place that is full, closely knit, abundant. Nature set down in ideal form. The two almost completed pictures, propped up on their stretchers, seem to overflow the barn as they will overflow men's minds and imaginations. Their titles will be *Spring* and *Summer* but they are infinitely more than that. They are all spring and all summer, each one a process of studious imagination brought to a conclusion that is inexhaustibly satisfying without ever being explained.[5] Because something has happened to Poussin, come over him practically unaware now that he is finishing. It will make Claude smile and shake his head when he finally sees these two paintings. For Poussin's extreme geometrical rigour, his exalted vision of intellectual design, has given rise in these last pictures to a strange look of foregone conclusion which is a most beautiful poetry. And poetry plus perfect form are unsurpassed.

In England there is a blind poet who sees with wonderful clarity the spring and summer that Poussin has imagined, at the same moment. In a torrent of incomparable, shining, magnificent language he states the same poetic argument of body and spirit in *Paradise Lost*.

In *Spring* (1660–64, Louvre) it is early morning. Poussin's luxuriant foliage partly conceals the geometry but exhibits in full view the problem of God in Milton's poem, the God who turns his back in the sky to permit the Fall, and the innocent tenderness of Adam and Eve.[6]

These, lull'd by nightingales, embracing slept,
And on their naked limbs the flow'ry roof
Show'r'd roses, which the morn repair'd.

Soon there is all the dreadful subtlety of the psychology of the Expulsion. You can imagine this Adam saying to himself:

How can I live without thee, how forgo
Thy sweet converse and love so dearly join'd,
To live again in these wild woods forlorn?

And hear Eve's desperate request for mercy:

bereave me not,
Whereon I live, thy gentle looks, thy aid,
Thy counsel in this uttermost distress,
My only strength and stay: forlorn of thee,
Whither shall I betake me, where subsist?

But here this ravishing tree and fruit-filled paradise is on the very point of being lost. The poem has the same unassailable grandeur of style as the painting and, like it, suggests a great deal more than it states.

All this and then Poussin's great final poem of a picture called *Summer*, done when he was beginning to feel unwell and to long for death, in which it is noon, with its golden gravity constructed block by block in the following way. Three figures in the foreground, shown in profile as though in a bas relief. Ruth kneels before Boaz. Beyond them, walls of corn treated as though they are rock or architecture, with the architectural detail on them of individual stems. The whole of the centre of the painting a passage of cornfield, archetypal, which progresses in recession towards distant mountains via a cliff with buildings on it, a bridge, rocks, an inlet, taking in as it goes the isolated incidents of reapers in the form of an extended frieze. One reaper quenches her thirst, one plays a bagpipe; women prepare bread in the shade of a tree; and, most beautiful of all, a Roman group of five horses is shown in classical style, all beneath a lit-up cloud.

Why should this be so heartbreakingly lovely? Its profound harmony between verticals and long horizontals, its reticence of style, the way in which it seems to set out something complicated with perfect simplicity, its understated grandeur, its marvellous use of light and colour, the way in which it balances the real and the ideal?[7]

All these. But something else as well which satisfies the mind and makes you think both of the ancient past and of the future, which, I am relieved to say, will not go into words. Something half remembered, hoped for or once dreamed.

Poussin has yet to complete the other two seasons, though *Autumn* is well advanced. But all four, with a room to themselves in the Louvre, have changed everything. Constable, Corot and, of course, Cézanne never got over their beauty or stopped seeing the world in terms of them. In time.

South Asia, with a population of 1.8 billion, battled successive waves of infection. In India and Pakistan there were thousands of deaths each day, and enormous death tolls continued to mount in North and South America.

Then the birds competed in ever louder singing in their separate territories. Bullfinches, goldfinches and chaffinches in the orchard. A song thrush at the top of a pear tree. Cock pheasants sounding their klaxons in the long grass. Moorhens pucking as they picked their way tidily about among the waterlilies. The cockerel crowing in the hen run all day, and the congenial afternoon conversations of geese. Only the white-faced barn owl remained silent, on its dignity at the door of the dovecot.

Columns of cumulus mounted their slow displays. Nothing of more stupendous beauty could be imagined than the bubbling up of bright peaks, sometimes smudged with little foreground puffs of smart French grey against the blue.

Goya

It is April 2nd, 1828, in Bordeaux, in a house on Cours de Tourny. Early morning. The Spaniard wakes and finds that he cannot move. He is aged eighty-two, a refugee.

In his head, a mule and a man are going down into Fuendetodos, the place in Aragon where he was born. The village looks derelict, as if no one lives there now. The heat, even to him, is oppressive. Completely still, airless heat, just as he remembers it. There is not much colour in the houses or even in the roofs because of the sun, which turns everything to white or pale ashes. The rooms look empty. Even the chapel is shuttered up. In his head he walks beside the *burro*, which is exhausted. From here he can see his house, the house in which he was born. He expects to see his mother. She will be as she was, still young. It is a pleasant sensation to him, now that he is dying, the anticipation of seeing his mother again, still young, and of walking towards her down the stone street of his childhood village in Aragon, despite the heat.

He has the confused, emotional feeling that you get in your head after a disturbing journey, or after the bullfight, or after war. It has been a long and dangerous journey. I would believe anything now, he thinks, including nightmares. Everything has become unreal and seems not to have consequences. There has been much violence. He knows that. And much blood, much dying. A dead person in Spain is more alive when he is dead, when the drunk priests sing and the Catholic angel drags his wings of rusty blades along the ground. In the mass a God is sacrificed. In the *duende* the true religious liturgy is the drama in which the bull is sacrificed. A bereavement for which there is no solace. Losing a person, like losing a musical instrument. Where do you stop and the world begin? The fervour of death's house. Now the mules are brought running into the ring and, the legs of the dead horses having been tied together, the mules drag the dead horses quickly across the sand and out of the ring, through the *barrera*. Sometimes the beautiful, wasp-waisted, fiery but not very intelligent, aristocratic whore of Seville will hide her long black hair in order to enter the convent.

He tries to breathe as evenly and slowly as possible and to keep his head. He sees very many people in his memory, their smiles and dead-fish eyes quickly brushed in with *bocetismo*, extreme sketchiness, but vividly enough that they are entirely real. It is possible he was happy when there were the extensive picnics with *majos* and *majas* and Madrid spread out pink beyond the Manzanares, when there were exaggerated, costumed characters at the fair and travelling people taught him caterwauling *tiranas*, folk songs. The fervent support of the bullfight enthusiasts for the matadors Costillares or Romero. The little court of Don Luis when the infante was an old man, out at Arenas de San Pedro, with Don Luis sitting at the table with his playing cards on it and Doña Maria Teresa having her hair dressed. Always the long black hair. And his paintings of children, of little Count de Altimira with his magpie on a string and the cats watching hungrily. Yes, he had shown a certain tenderness then in his paintings of the children who were beautiful in their way and would come to grief, in their marriages and politically. A tenderness he had tended to keep well hidden in the rest of his work, except sometimes when painting Aragonese, his friends from Aragon.

But it was also a terrible time, when all his own children died except for Francisco Xavier – and you can never be more happy than your least happy child, and no amount of friendship with the tottering king and his mastiffs, and the putting a *de* in his name to show that he has gone up in the world and the acquisition of a *birlocho*, a stylish carriage which he very soon turned over. None of that could make up for the fact that his Enlightenment friends and patrons like Don Gaspar Melchor de Jovellanos and the old noble families were destroyed by the queen's lover, Manuel Godoy, who became a prince and controlled everything. And then there was the French occupation and the terrible events of May 2–3, 1808, in Madrid, when his friends the Bales family were assassinated. He knew, in a confused way, it should have been this that he saw in his mind's eye, but in fact what he is seeing now is the normalizing of evil, the dreadful split between political identity and the animal, which is just the body, just meat, and is entirely superfluous, to be disposed of like a flea. The difference between how you think and how you live. Had he been able to move on his bed he would have flailed in despair at the terror, the cruelty.

And then, of course, he begins to think of the state's illness in conjunction with his own illness, his sickness and his lovesickness. These are confused in his head because of the funeral of the Duke of Alba in Madrid coming between his own infatuation with the Duke's widow before it and just after it in Sanlúcar de Barrameda, and how he painted the Duchess in mourning with his own name all over her before he came to understand that she had no feelings for him whatever and was only amusing herself, and that the opposite of love is not hate but indifference. Indifference, because he was fifty and she was thirty-four. And his passion for her had contributed to his second and most terrible illness, in Cádiz, at the house of Don Sebastián Martínez, when the noises in his head became so appalling that all the shutters of his mind burst open and, when he was finally able to work again, he could no longer hear, and caprice and invention were as actual to him as what he knew to be real. Nightmares and the macabre flapped up in his face. And from now on, whether he was syphilitic, schizophrenic or paranoid, physical illness combined with mental suffering would, in his head, all become part of war and the Inquisition.

Strange and dreadful, the events he thinks of then, figures halfway between reality and fantasy. The queen Maria Luisa's hat *incroyable*, aping that of Marie Antoinette, her horse called Marcial, and the joke he played by putting an anonymous woman in the great royal portrait. Who is she, she who turns away, standing next to the future Ferdinand VII? They all ask that.

You cannot see her face. And now they will never know. Ha! He smiles inwardly. But not for long, because of the indiscriminate killing of Madrileños, residents of Madrid, in the vicinity of the Montaña del Príncipe Pío, and the brutality and violence of the new kind of war in which ordinary country people try to assist the professional armies of the Spanish and British by harassing the French, resulting in the most cruel acts of vengeance and reprisal. The beleaguered populations of Girona and Zaragoza were put through hell and terrible tortures, some of which he saw or had explained to him by eyewitnesses in writing and mime, so that he could draw and etch the atrocities with absolute veracity. All of it is confused with the flagellants and the conical hats of the Inquisition, the giant in his house of the deaf man, his black paintings and the terrible death of the mayor of Torrejón, gored by a bull that broke out of the ring. And then there is the famine and the country already ruined, racked by poverty after six years of war and with a corrupt government. His Spain. His Spain. And, lying here paralysed, he cannot even twitch.

So what does he do, thinking of the unremitting sun, when the dream of reason produces monsters and he has finally finished ridiculing vices, prejudices, follies, women, lawyers, physicians, priests? *Sol, sol y sombra, sombra.* And for years he has been unable to hear the screaming, only the screaming in his head, and the dancers are all quite drunk and it is necessary to shout, presumably because of the noise of the fiesta, with the jokers going about in the crowd, hitting people with their bladders. Once, people thought of him as the master of greys and silvers. Now he can picture no emotion without the possibility of death. The sand-laden winds of the mind. So what does he do? What finally does he do, this long-deaf artist who has seen love, atrocity, madness and illness at close quarters and now finds himself to be over eighty?

I think I can tell you. He sees old age as part of the fiesta, its pratfalls and indignities as part of a procession of cruel jokes and general hilarity. What is funnier than tumbling down stairs, than forgetting your own name, than finding you are married to the woman you most feared, than trying to carry your own mule, than failing utterly to dance the bolero or stand on your head when you feel the need of it? You were famous for your beauty, now you are ugly. Your laughter was delightful, now you can do nothing but shriek and cackle. You passionately loved your sister's husband, now he is a goat or turkey. The slights you endured, the grudges you held, the feuds you kept up, all have escaped you.

I would not be too dogmatic about the last part: what is in his head and what is out of it. Can he sign? Can he finger-spell in Spanish? Does he know any French? Can he lip-read? He finds himself in Bordeaux with a much younger woman, his last mistress, Leocadia Zorrilla de Weiss, who is violent and with whom he argues. His son, whom he loves, has become fat and almost unrecognizable. All his old friends are dead.

In Bordeaux an enormous woman is carried piggyback. An amputee tries to wheel himself along. An old man tries to unpadlock a girl. A penitent is on his knees. A man attempts to de-flea his dog. He draws them all. Sometimes you come to a town and half the inhabitants are deaf. Blood drips on the table from some dead thing hanging up. The devil's wings are on someone's back, and a noisy coven of Fates is invariably in the shadows. A monk screams without sound. And there are always the old, including himself, to laugh at. The old women dance in the air, playing cymbals, castanets and guitars. People tumble down stairs, are incontinent, seduce each other, forget each other and themselves, confuse each others' children, take inappropriate pleasures. A toothless grinner is working a swing. Who is to say that all the old people are not him? He grows a sticking-out beard. His ankles hurt. Forgets what he was going to say. Feels a fool on sticks. The king's *pintor de cámara*, official court painter. He laughs. He is always learning. What are they saying about him that he cannot hear? How ridiculous, life!

I hope he saw his mother again when he and the *burro* went back in his head to Fuendetodos.

A fortnight is used up in thoughts like these, and on April 16th, 1828, at two a.m., he dies. At first he is buried in Bordeaux. Of course he must go back to Spain, and in 1901 his body is exhumed and reburied in the chapel of San Antonio de la Florida, which he once decorated, in Madrid. But when his body is exhumed, the head, as a last joke, is missing – the head in which all this happened. And only the rest of him, in the end, goes home.

Velázquez's *Las Meninas*

Perhaps it was the itinerant people clapping irregular rhythms and singing in high voices, or the legless man wheeling himself around on a tray, that made me think to tell you of how death also hides in Velázquez's great *Las Meninas*, though I only mention it in passing.

With difficulty, workmen have unhooked the chandeliers in a large room on the ground floor facing across the palace square in the Alcázar, to make it into a workshop for Velázquez. It is 1656. For more than thirty years he has been painting Philip IV, almost his only patron, and now he is starting on a big picture of the most inordinate originality and concealed cunning. Its chief subject is the king's favourite infanta, Margarita Teresa, who is five. She will die aged twenty-one after seven pregnancies. The *menina* on her left is Maria Sarmiento, who will die within two years. The woman with dwarfism is German, though she is called Maribárbola. The man on the steps is Velázquez's friend José Nieto, a court official. The king and queen appear foggily in the mirror. But Velázquez, who looks past the canvas. What is it that he does not yet know?

Excuse me if I pause to point out how all these figures are set in a structure. The group is shown fairly far forward in the room, with a beautiful, gloomy space behind it. Apart from the burst of light at the back there are two light sources, one immediately to the right of the viewer and another which throws a diagonal strip of sunlight across the floor towards the rear wall. Then there are triangles. These triangles are set up by the stretcher of the canvas, the brushes and mahlstick, and Nicolasito Pertusato with his foot on the dog to the right. There is also, of course, an implied triangle running backwards into the space and another coming forward to include you, the viewer, within the firm cube of the room. But that is not all. Now think of the whole group as seen from above. This puts the infanta's round dress near the middle of a series of other circles. But even that is not quite all, because there remains the central device or conceit of the picture, which is the mirror. When you look at the painting, its bottom edge is so low down that the mat on the artist's floor appears to be a continuation of the floor on which you stand. But the whole group turns towards the king and queen, who must surely be standing where the artist stands; that is, where the viewer stands. So, if the canvas in the picture is this painting, the implication is that the whole group is seen in a mirror.

I have tried to describe the painting's cleverness but find myself speechless at its beauty. Like many people, I had my mind altered about life by seeing it in a way from which I have never recovered. The same happened when I saw Piero della Francesca's *Madonna del Parto* (c. 1460), in its little shedlike Tuscan chapel at Monterchi (as it was then, while the bored guide waited, smoking, outside). That is why I mention *Las Meninas* here, because it is a supreme example of what turned out to be late style. All I can do is say that it shows a condemned child in trappings of grandeur when the royal family was extremely insecure and the court bankrupt.

Velázquez's technique is spectacularly free. In this picture it has an exhilarating breadth, almost a roughness, combined with nervous control which produces tension. The drawing is superb, especially across almost bare areas in which it makes use of the nap of the canvas and thinned pigment. The whole big machine still somehow comes as a surprise and is full of panache, invention and psychological insight in a structure that directly includes the viewer. I can say all this but my remarks add up to very little. In the end the picture is both heartbreakingly beautiful and a complete mystery.

And Velázquez? What does he not know? That he has very nearly come to the end. He shows himself in the picture as the intimate of the royal family, at the height of his powers and still relatively young. In fact, he is fifty-seven and dies soon afterwards. He lies in state for a time in his bedroom in the robes of a knight of Santiago.

The wonder of the picture's construction has so fascinated the king that, having followed its progress with attention, he keeps it to himself in his study as soon as it is finished. He dies a broken man in 1665, and the room in which the picture was painted is burned down in 1734. But Velázquez's mighty painting is in the Prado when it opens in 1819. Later it is shown there in an otherwise empty room, with a large mirror facing it.

A Footnote about El Greco

Toledo. Under that torn sky. The green of the Tajo below, and the jagged grey line of the city wall like a brushstroke on the escarpment. If, going from church to monastery to his house, you look for his last paintings, you will notice the following: that he paints with alarming speed, that he paints always on a warm brown ground, and that he deliberately damages faces towards the end of a painting, perhaps out of exuberance. On the backs of many of the late single-figure pictures and all around the portraits there are splashes and brushmarks, hidden by the frame, where he tests his colours, using the brown ground as a palette. The portraits, ostensibly of saints and apostles, include what seem to be many self-portraits, an old face with the same pointed, grizzled beard. And the further eye, when the head is seen in three-quarter view, the eye on the shadowed side, is often damaged by a single, dark, excitable, vertical brushstroke that simultaneously blinds it and brings it astonishingly to life. Beyond is the scorched bull's hide of the Castilian plain. Thirty-nine years El Greco spent here in these narrow streets, up and down these steps under the Moorish *puertas*, gateways, worn out by the grey-green of cacti and scarred agave. He came here first in 1577 to work in the ancient church of Santo Domingo el Antiguo. Go into this church now, and look through a hole in the floor of the nave, and you will see with a slight shock his small coffin on a table in the crypt, the coffin painted the same brown as his ground.

With the very hot weather came the butterflies. Sunlight and
nectar were a heady cocktail. Short lives were nothing but
dancing and activity. Colour was dust and dust was colour, the
brightest blue one side of a wing and an archipelago of brown
dots on the other. Different characters when open or closed. Only
the largest basked; the small ones sprang up and fluttered, all but
collided in their eagerness. They were dizzy, erratic, nervous fliers
in the lavender and in the wildflowers of the orchard, where they
worked with no apparent system, excitedly. Unrolled a proboscis.
Here was carmine. Here gamboge. Here the day's yellowest
lemon or a dab of black on white. Already moved on. No. There.

Poppies in clumps and scarlet swathes, their tissue-paper
petals and black eyeliner. Corn burnished in fields with vertical,
flat-sided edges. Soft shadows in trumpets of white convolvulus
where it had climbed hedges. Twerping and noisy outbursts
of house sparrows under the north jetty. Round bumble bees
changing places all day in enormous mounds of soft blue
lavender.

Morandi

An old city the colour of soap, cardboard, melon and cheese. Bologna, in Emilia-Romagna. A place of dusty bricks, almost no marble. In every street, shady arcades. The house in via Fondazza. Along the shady arcade to number 36 and up the steps, round two corners, to the apartment on the first floor. Time. It is any time between 1910 and 1964. The windows on the first floor look down into a courtyard and small garden at the back with an olive tree and the scar of a semicircular path with some flowerpots near it and the backs of some buildings holding shade. Once there was a factory and a factory chimney, and occasionally a factory siren hooted. At the end of the street there is a small, shady public garden with some pine trees and a mulberry, and a hard tennis court with high mesh round it. Or was that earlier? There is no one about because it is midday.

The farmland in the vicinity is bleached by the sun. A small train with an elderly locomotive, curtains flapping out of the windows, crosses the farmland, and from the train you can just see the sun-bleached houses of a tiny village on a slope above faded crops and the scorched mountains of the Bolognese Apennines, brown in the distance. Some events in the future become present and then recede into the past. The future lacks the reality of the past and present, so reality is continually being added to as time passes.

A bedroom at 36 via Fondazza has been fitted up, long ago, as a studio. It is a brick-floored room with a high ceiling and a shutter or screen made of hessian and gauze rigged up in the window to soften the sunlight. Also two shelves, one almost at eye level, the other much lower, on which to arrange still-life objects. Some sheets of off-white paper, fixed to the wall with drawing pins to make a backdrop or in some cases a horizon for the objects. Two easels with brushmarks on them. A table on which there are pencilled representations of the relative positions of objects, a sort of map of their changing positions. A second table with brushes and some tubes of oil paint on it. A low bed with a chair beside it.

In a small adjoining room a few books about Chardin, Corot, Cézanne, and two Rembrandt etchings.

And in a cupboard in the passage: a twisted white vase, a tin box with one side painted black, a fluted vase, an oil funnel, a little white bowl, a lamp with a long neck, a small stringed instrument (not quite a mandolin), a spiked shell and some speckled shells.

On a hook in the bedroom a paint-marked blue jacket and, in a corner, an old trilby and an umbrella.

It is hard to say whether Morandi has just left these rooms a moment ago or whether he has been away all summer in Grizzana.

There is the pleasant smell of bread. The Futurists used to say you cannot tell from looking at it whether the empty piazza was full a minute ago or whether there was a massacre in it last Wednesday. If it were 1942, Morandi would probably be in the rooms because of the war. If it were early in the day, one of his sisters, Anna, Dina or Maria Teresa, might have gone out to buy bread. We should not think of the present as moving along the sequence of events from past to future.

Morandi is abnormally tall, thin, angular, and somewhat shy. He does not say a great deal. He prefers to live very simply. It is possible he has taped up the plate of one of his drypoints in brown paper and taken it on the bus with him to the printer's near the river and the bread factory. The asymmetry of time is its most striking feature. Trees grow. Children become old. The ancient Greek equivalent of *be* is used in more than one way. The olive tree in the courtyard is much taller now, and Morandi as an old man is recognizably the serious boy who stands beside his father in a photograph of 1902. It is touching to see him in a family group, groups of objects being what he will paint, one object in front of another and then an interval between the next and the picture's edge. Old cartographers did not distinguish between distance and time, and the universe starts from a low state of entropy.

If it is July 1944 there are war planes in the blue sky above Grizzana because the defence line, Linea Gotica, is established very close to there; bombardments are audible and Morandi is back in Bologna. But if it is 1913 or 1927, or 1933, say, or any time between 1958 and 1964, the summers are the same, the buildings the same, the land the same and Morandi much the same, quietly painting them. Despite fascism, times unchanged, the district constant. A metaphysical solace, Nietzsche called it, the business of seeing things unaffected by the world's shifting, aside momentarily from movement and whirl. The flat, interlocking patches of pale colour which Morandi observes in the countryside are subdued by the heat-haze.

From the outset, he knew that he could say what he had to say by painting still lifes, the occasional flower piece and the local landscape. It was a peculiarly old-fashioned thing to do in a period of modernism, but the seriousness and intensity of his work meant that there was no question of Morandi being repetitive, any more than Chardin was repetitive. Each painting, even if it is made up of the same objects as countless others, is a fresh and lively solution to a new problem, a new set of circumstances and a changed condition. The sadness of a few objects on a table, or the elation when they come together, is expressed as if for the first time. There are years when things huddle together with much space around them, others when they seek to make a line and stand separate, others when they get in one another's way. The shelf is the land. Sometimes there is no horizon. What they are dependent on, these pictures, is a curious kind of thought made up largely of the geometry of intuition. Objects and the intervals between them are scrutinized as sensations in the artist's mind, tried this way and that, until a vibration or a little visual surprise seems valid, and then set down as clearly and straightforwardly as possible. Brushmarks, paint scrubbed in to cover open areas, suggest that in the end pictures are painted quite quickly. For these are a series of answers that have been arrived at to questions asked sometimes a long time ago.

Time. If it were 1914 he would be teaching drawing in local elementary schools. If it were 1930, he would be embarking on a twenty-six-year stint as professor of etching and engraving at Bologna Academy. Yet nothing much changes. In his room, the same bottles, jars, boxes and jug await him on his marked table, and he still finds them and their calm a puzzle and a consolation from the convolutions of the outside world. And each summer he still spends four months at Grizzana, the village he first visited in 1913, to paint the surrounding landscape. How can I convey to you the nature of this sameness?

In time. Parts of S. Stefano, in Bologna, are from the 6th century. In the university there is still the oldest anatomical theatre in Europe. The little medieval shops in via Pescherie Vecchie and via Clavature still sell produce from the valleys of the Po and the Reno as they have always done. The astonishing *torri*, Asinelli and Garisenda, still touch the sky like Morandi's bottles. And the biscuit-yellow crops and distant clumps and barns which he observes from his window at Grizzana have not changed either. Which summer was that? The year when a pattern of trees was apparent between two barns the colour of bone. The one when some brown fields were divided by a pinkish-grey rise in the ground. Events in the landscape take place in much the same way that they occur in still lifes, as, for instance, when three white utensils permitted to appear beyond them the dark red-brown of a swollen vase. Morandi is the post-cubist Chardin.

To remain as consistent as this, it is essential to him that he goes away from Bologna as little as possible. Once, when he was in his mid-twenties, he went to Rome to meet de Chirico, who proclaimed the eternal laws of geometry to be the basis of all great beauty and profound melancholy. And twice he went to Venice and felt out of place. In 1956 he ventured to Zurich to see a Cézanne exhibition. But that was all. He needed all the time he could get, gently to alter the colours of the familiar objects he was studying by painting on their surfaces. And he needed time, propping his spectacles on his forehead, for his philosophical meditations on the ways in which, in landscape, boundaries separate one thing from another.

But then, of course, someone with no sense of humour moved the hands forward on the stopped clock, and Morandi was suddenly old. The same youthful man, but old. He stopped teaching in 1956 and began at once to work out his late idea, almost as if he had only just got going. Some great artists in old age are pristine, hopeful, inspired, and full of bounteous surprises. Nearly all his watercolours were done in the last eight years of his life, and half his drawings in the last four. There was also an enormous increase, a positive outpouring, of his paintings based on landscape. It was as if he was curious to see what would transpire. Perhaps the remission of difficulties made him happy.

In all this late work he went much further than before. It was as if his conscious and subconscious ran ahead in ecstasy, by instinct. This is all but impossible to write about. His subject was still the steadfastness of the visible world but now it was reduced to very little, almost to nothing. Forms are built up in wonderful, almost colourless, puddles of shade. Intervals themselves often become a subject and much of his page or canvas is left bare. Some of the most beautiful watercolours seem only to consist of light, incorporating the whiteness of the paper, with a line that indicates both contour and shadow at the same time. The truth, when it finally makes its appearance, is often simple, almost incidental, like a by-product or miraculous accident. It is the unstated in art which sometimes encapsulates its meaning. We seem to be in an area between standing forms that has to do with a higher state of existence and with spiritual values.

Perhaps there is one clue to how this comes about in Morandi's way of observing landscape. When at Grizzana he does not paint outside but looks from his windows, using binoculars and sometimes even a telescope. This has the effect of isolating distant details of countryside in the summer haze, simplifying contrasts of colour and of light and shade into something of the geometric solidity of a landscape background by Piero. Hence the glassy air, the vines hardly green, the blue and brown of the slopes, the band of dust that is a whitish road, the glimpsed cube of a barn. And, of course, the tranquillity.

So what does this leave? By the time he is seventy the familiar motifs are reduced to little more than fractions of their former selves, essences. They become minimal observations so tender and clear that they barely touch the page. There is the shade, the angle, the gap, the absence, the masking and the constant light. But there is also an unimpeachable harmony that has about it something permanent and profound.

Somehow Morandi instructs us in an odd poetry, a certain equilibrium from within, which we recognize at once but cannot explain. The strange, infinitely strange, business of a rendezvous with intelligibility. It is a beautiful thing to see, in a landscape or among his utensils, this vestige of something already known, an awareness of something predating our own consciousness perhaps, which is intense and lasting, and quite unrelated to its stature. Just as music is time organized, the sudden inrush of meaning in a modest work by Morandi brings us within an ace of knowing something normally estranged from our condition, and yet something we long for. Entering the painting is like coming home. Death and its vast perspectives have a way of dwarfing all that is of no importance.

And time? We make little enough effort to understand time until we have lost it. You think time passes? Not so, says Morandi from his old landscape and his old city the colour of soap, cardboard, melon, cheese and dust. Places and pictures last. Time remains. It is we who pass.

A question of numbers. Numbers of those in hospital, those infected, contagious, condemned. The numbers of those unburied. Percentages and estimates. Comparisons of death rates between countries and between continents. A gasping new form of arithmetic which calculates in corpses and reckons in rates of infection. News of the world's suffering is expressed in almost nothing but numbers.

Opposite to this is: the solidity of objects.

Now the kitchen door stands open to extensive birdsong and strong sunlight. Inside there are brick floors, stone sinks, slate, lead, pottery and utensils, jars of flowers, baskets and wire mesh racks of vegetables. The small sounds of a petal opening, a wasp rasping on wood, the nervous ticking of the kitchen clock with 'Thornbury' written on it. Tacked to the matchboard walls are flower-show prize certificates for roses, apples, tarts, preserves, an out-of-date calendar, a dog-eared postcard of a Maillol sculpture, a woodcut of a plant, a photograph of Mrs Frawley in an apron preparing onions and cauliflowers. On a shelf a row of stained cookbooks. Also such paperbacks as *Keeping Poultry and Rabbits on Scraps*.

It is a kitchen and scullery full of firm, architectural objects, well worn, satisfying to hold, redolent with usefulness: colander, sieve, grater, crock, mincing machine, jelly mould, funnel, pudding bowl. A lesser world of saucepans, wooden spoons, stacked weights and iron scales, Kilner jars, stoves, heating pipes and pie dishes. Into it sometimes venture chickens, pecking about and perching, unaware of numbers, on wooden draining boards.

Chardin

You would not think, seeing Chardin as an old man crossing rue des Orties on his way back to his apartment in the Louvre, that a drawer opened for its shadow would strike him as poetic. A moderate man, Chardin. Orderly, with a good grasp of his pension and allowances. Thrifty with materials and an excellent craftsman. In charge of hanging Salon exhibitions, which inevitably provokes a few antagonisms, but he and the second Madame Chardin live comfortably enough and modestly in four rooms full of rosewood furniture, ragout spoons and frock coats. But poetry? Who would have thought that such a man, who now suffers from a gallstone and has developed an aversion to the smell of oil paint, would see the importance of a playing-card's shadow on green baize?

Green baize and well-made tables and cabinets. His father made billiard tables, and for years Chardin lived in rue Princesse with his brother, Juste, a master cabinetmaker. It is very quiet. The furniture stands well, and you could build a card-house on it with the moral obligation to make things as simple and orderly as possible. Equilibrium and sanity. A quiet commitment to bringing order and humanity into a world threatened very soon by disorder and revolution.

As he crosses rue des Orties, he looks up. There is a humming noise. The too-loud humming noise of a swarm of bees or locusts? *Tische*. A pane of glass shatters in a first-floor window. In a side street, between grand architecture, he glimpses a crowd of struggling figures.

To make life more bearable with a sane and natural art, Chardin has developed a self-defence against the future. Not everyone understands this, that you need to recognize and somehow fix objects before they are snatched away from you for ever, before the table trembles and the card-house falls down.

It has to do, this basket of strawberries or jar of olives, with memory and loss. I shall have hours of pleasure, thinks this moderate man, if I study the biography of a slice of melon, a brioche or a jug of freesias under the light. There is no hurry. It takes time. People think him idle at various points in his career because he produces no more than a picture a year, but he does not paint particularly slowly. Look closely at the grand and simple architecture of the pictures and you see that, with a certain breadth of handling, they alter the world rather than seeking to copy it. Painting about paradise is to do with being overwhelmed. Somehow, with human scale and warmth, he must remember what he felt when he first saw an object, and then make an equivalent. Everything depends on handling and the artist's hand.

And so objects, as recognized in due course by Morandi and de Chirico and in the first place by Giotto, have a presence and express a meaning beyond their physical appearance. As he gets older, Chardin sets them at eye level on shelves, ledges, tables, almost always on dark grounds. In the world of pure painting, this is the metaphysics of the everyday object. It leads Proust to remark that a pear painted by Chardin is as much alive as a woman. It is fortunate, although it always annoys him, that Chardin lacks the education to be a history painter. The nearest he comes is painting his servant, Marie-Anne Cheneau, leaning on her broom, or Auguste-Gabriel Godefroy in a child's tricorn hat, but instead his essential and profound subject becomes an intuitive experiment with things, perfectly ordinary things, and the spaces between them, and that is more than enough.

Shuttlecocks. Apricots. Objects stand in front of one another, reverse each other's silhouettes and profiles and very slightly reflect each other's colours. Tolstoy says that structure and significance, essential to art, are utterly absent from life. Chardin goes up to his room and puts on his nightcap and eyeshade. May as well be comfortable. His only aching sadness is that he has alienated his son, Jean-Pierre, over money. Pruinescence on a plum. The wriggle of a walnut's construction. The intimacy and big stillness of a jug. He insists on a daily shave. Vollard will get into trouble in 1900 when he suggests that still lifes by Cézanne and Chardin are concerned with the same things and should be shown side by side. He is right. By 1760, just when his sales start to tail off, Chardin finds a way to treat all things as divinely equal.

You can see how he arrives at a beautiful unity by marking pictures quite broadly all over, with great spontaneity. He draws across the whole canvas in burnt ultramarine or with the remains of some white, sometimes (Diderot says) using his thumb, and in the process gives extraordinary density and fullness to forms, with what seems to be complete ease of handling. Sometimes that scumbled mark becomes the roughness of pottery, the glint on the meniscus in a glass of water, the shine on a cherry or the fur on a peach. Living is less important than remembering. The poetry. And when a single carmine brushmark suggests a fallen petal, almost as though he is cleaning his brush towards the bottom edge of the canvas, the world is transformed, and it turns your heart over.

The dance of death continued and I began to think of the day in late June 1813 when John Constable got down from a cart in East Bergholt village street, in the borders of Suffolk and Essex, and walked up to his father's house in perfect weather.

Half a lifetime ago, when it was first possible to get a facsimile of the little sketchbook he had in his pocket that afternoon, I did what countless other people have done and went to find his places. The sketchbook was 3½ by 4¾ inches and contained seventy-two pages. On foot and by rowing boat, in fine weather, I spent several weeks identifying much of what he had seen. And each evening I went back to a big old farmhouse with grouped brick chimneys which he had drawn one Sunday morning from the lane. He noted it was a Sunday morning on the drawing. My bedroom there was bare and simple and its windows overlooked a row of chestnut trees and there was the constant grating of guinea fowl.

Constable's late style was waiting then, of course, impatiently half hidden, as it does in all of us. But to begin with, before loss and depression and the passage of time got to work on the way in which he saw, there was a world in the drawings of sunlit views and soft gradations.

Constable

That summer of 1813 is the warmest of the 19th century and people remember it long afterwards for its incomparable wheat harvests.

Constable is thirty-six. Everything he sees at East Bergholt stands unchanged since his childhood. The pink-faced foursquare house, East Bergholt House, in which he was born. His parents. His mother's flower garden. The kitchen garden, with Mr Prestney at work in the heat among the vegetables and cutting borders. His friend John Dunthorne the plumber's workshop in the centre of the village. Miss Taylor's school. The productive and orderly surrounding farmland. The river Stour, canalized for barges. His father's watermills at Flatford and Dedham.

From his bedroom window at the top of the house he can see Bergholt windmill, in which he worked for a year when he was sixteen, the paths he walked with Maria Bicknell and the rectory of her obstructive grandfather, Dr Rhudde. It has taken Constable since he was twenty to realize that, in an age of references and connections, all he needs to do is to draw and paint this place straightforwardly, truthfully, and to try to forget that he has ever seen another picture.

Time, it does but pass. Perhaps he senses that the indefinable, the oddly inexpressible part of this landscape, will follow if he can but set down one fact truthfully.

In the sketchbook drawings he produces over the next three months there are small accents of dark in clumps of shadow. The drawings are either done in the village or no more than a short walk away, with three longer excursions by trap to Chelmsford, Colchester and Mistley. He draws the distant tower of Stoke-by-Nayland church, Glebe Farm at Langham, wide views of Dedham Vale. A barge goes under Stratford Old Bridge. There is, drawn many times, the porch of East Bergholt church, the tower of Stratford St Mary. In perfect reticence, a peaceful land. No haste. The weather holds. A donkey stretches up to eat a hedge. There are gaps between elms, reaches of tranquil river, tents, poplars, small figures on roads, a full moon, a lark above standing corn. A village fair. A rainbow.

Occasionally he breaks off to paint in oils on only a slightly larger scale because he needs also to catch the incomparable freshness and brightness of the morning or an afternoon with the river bank in deep shadow. Next to the clock on East Bergholt church tower is inscribed, in Latin, *As a shadow, so is life*. Waiting in the heat above the cottages is a King James Bible countryside, full of reminders not to waste time and to watch. *O that they were wise, that they understood this, that they would consider their latter end! –* Deuteronomy. *Blessed is the man that heareth me, watching daily at my gates, waiting at the posts of my doors –* Proverbs.

On these days it is necessary to trap the light and it is in Constable's nature to do this. In the smallest pencil drawings he catches the shade, but in the little oil sketches or *pochardes* done in the lid of his paintbox since 1809, with the clearest and most sensitive of palettes, he knows how to catch the sunlight on a sweep of lawn or below an active sluice with a marvellous alertness to the dash or smear of a coloured mark.

A succession of smudges is the elder in bloom near the wall of Willy Lott's house. A single clear brushmark puts reflected light suddenly into the water by the bridge. A group of tall trees which share the same rounded top hold rich shadow in a green made darker and more beautiful by a battery of animated scrubbings that seem almost accidental. If the diminutive sketchbook drawings catch the appearance of things, the little oil sketches joyfully catch their atmosphere. Such sketches are the more wonderful and the more precious for their spontaneity, small size and apparent simplicity of means. Sometimes they look almost cursory. Incidental. English countryside in a few breathtaking touches by an artist whose technique and whole mentality are caught up in utter pleasure at the view.

So this is to be the summer which lasts and lasts in the present but is already in the past.

What is it to be well and then not well? To be the person you are and then the one you have become?

Two years later, Constable's mother falls down in the new round bed she has been making in her flower garden. A stroke. She dies in 1815. His father dies soon afterwards. Bergholt House is sold, and then demolished. In 1816 the sun goes behind a cloud of volcanic particles and does not come out for a year. Crops fail. There is no longer any summer.

Now I will try to show you what happens to his painting as the cloud goes over his psyche and the shadow damages him. The shadow, that is, of life's normal cruelty. During the next twenty years he becomes a London studio painter dependent on visits to the country, on old open-air drawings and oil sketches and on a most powerful longing.

He marries Maria Bicknell after an interminable engagement and realizes that she is falling ill. She once wrote to him asking, 'I wonder which you have thought of most this summer, landscape or me?' The apparently carefree small pictures that he paints of the seashore at Brighton are only done because they have come there for her health and she is lying in a room on the front, unable to breathe. Then the rain falls into the sea. His long struggle with the Royal Academy goes on, epitomized by the denigration of a watermeadow picture by him, by the selection committee, when he is present in the room. The truth is that for years academicians cannot bring themselves to elect a landscape painter and he is too proud to defend himself. When Maria dies, not only is he inconsolable but he is left with seven children under twelve years old to look after. When his great friend and only real supporter, John Fisher, and Johnny Dunthorne die within weeks of each other, winter, his unfamiliar season, enters his soul. From then on, in the 1830s, he begins often to get ill himself and temporarily loses the use of his right hand.

Painting done in distress unlocks some stupendous revisions. Constable is once asked by a truculent younger academician why he does not sell more pictures and he explains as follows: 'I am reluctant to let the less good pictures go, and the best I like always to keep around me.' In truth he is an inveterate reviser and, if he has the work in the studio, he will often revisit it.

With Maria no longer in the world, he sees it as totally changed. His first conviction, that if he tells the truth about appearances their meaning will follow, no longer applies. Now it is not just countryside and buildings that the pictures must convey. There needs in some inexplicable way to be a charge or a peculiar significance in their handling which holds the meaning itself. His handling becomes impatient. Paint which used to go on easily now seems sometimes to require more working and the passages of effortless sparkle will not always come. The strange reconfiguration which happens when a palette begins to work, when colour within colour takes on a curious life of its own, no longer seems to materialize. Until, that is, the whole notion of what he is doing is reinvented by him in the pigment.

There are clear signs from now on of brushing, scraping and wiping with a flexible knife over already existing paint. In the last work the handling overwhelms appearances and, mixing/throwing/overpainting/scraping/hinting/cancelling and restating, it makes an impatient bid for a state of mind. There is a dance of marks. Almost a need to scribble. Stirring white pigment into more white pigment, he leaves the eye and mind all but blinded. In this way the painting itself becomes the subject and is no longer constrained by appearances. Appearances are from now on in the chance mark, the chance remark, the splash and the smudge, as much as in the clouds and in the interrupted air. Do you really want me, he asks, to block every appearance with facts? No, I want the double rainbow, the moorhen frightened across weeds, the drench of elderflower.

When you stand up close to these passages they are terrifying. Seen at a distance they take your imagination into a place of exhilaration. What is already high in tone is kneaded and stretched with energy until it radiates brightness and everything else is lowered by contrast.

Think what painting can do when it has all the appearance of one world but turns out to have all the characteristics of quite another. 'Finish! Finish!' people said to Constable as his paintings seemed to them to become rougher and rougher, but what they failed to realize was that the degree of meaning he was so determined to convey only existed in apparently incomplete form. The marks that some critics said looked like chopped straw or dripped household paint are part of a heartfelt attempt to reach past the subject to something else which is unique to painting, the curious fusion of actuality and idea or paint and sensation. This takes place in extreme circumstances, often when the painter is not entirely sure of his ground. A matter of risk. When visited on already existing paintings it can gain in subtlety because it has the spontaneity of a sketch on something that already has the gravitas of a thought-out statement. I think this is largely what painting is. No wonder, when Delacroix eventually saw these later pictures, he understood their point immediately. It is not just the lifelong attempt to paint the dew on the grass. It is a state of flux which makes all the old pain of time and altered condition into a throb of paint which will not be explained.

When Maria dies there is a long period of intense grief that stops him working entirely. In the end it is quite a slight drawing from fifteen years earlier, done at Hadleigh in Essex, of a tower overlooking the Thames estuary, that unlocks him from his dreadful stasis.

It is a split, black tower.

'Je suis le Ténébreux, – le Veuf, – l'Inconsolé' (I am the man of
shadows, – the widower, – the unconsoled, the disconsolate)
– Gérard de Nerval

Constable's pain goes into the paint. He breaks his rule and moves the architecture about, realigning it so that the masonry impedes the light. In the six-foot-wide sketch for this picture there is a beautiful tantrum of painting in a passage of reworked sky. The tapper of the glass, the artist who put the time and date on clouds and kept an eye on barometric pressure all his life, now shows the sky not scientifically but as blue air roiling in his mind.

In the last great Salisbury painting, *Salisbury Cathedral from the Meadows* (1831, Tate), an arc that has been waiting, coiled, in the lower left-hand corner of the picture expands into one of the most resplendent and majestic of all his compositions with the addition of a late rainbow. It is not there when he draws and paints the cathedral from the north-west, near Fisherton's Mill, at the outset. Like the clouds, like life itself, it occurs and then fades out in almost no time.

Finally, debarred from them by more than years and distance, he revisits in his head his places when the days were fair. I cannot tell you, he seems to say, exactly what it was but in a last moment before the birth of consciousness it passed, much missed and pined for, passed and passed away. Redolent of such joy is the sky above *The Leaping Horse* sketch (c. 1825, V&A, London) and the moment when the hare runs out and scatters time locked in the antique stillness of the stones in a late Stonehenge watercolour. And in the East Bergholt cottages. There is the little one with a rainbow at odds with its chimney's plume of smoke and its foreground ploughed by the butt of the brush. And the superb late picture in which, trapped in a thicket of shadow, the cottage is turned and tilted by a gust of feeling. This, surely, is the cottage, never as then, that stood by the Fen Lane path he took to school to learn his Latin and passed often in happier times in a continuous present. And now in his invented weather.

There is to be no autumn. Constable really only paints one autumnal picture, when he makes the Coleorton stag and cenotaph refer to Titian's *Death of Actaeon* with all the temporary colours of a quince.

He dies unexpectedly, aged sixty. The Academy decides that his last picture, of the mill below Arundel, is sufficiently finished to show. In it, white water bubbles into brown.

Now came a period when, because of the heat, I lived in the garden more than ever. Normally cool rooms became hard to work in so I wrote outside, bathed in a pond and slept in an old bell tent, or in a hammock slung between two trees. There were sunflowers, runner beans, sweet peas, the first figs and first honey, and the long summer was without guile. The Lombardy poplars quivered in the heat. It amused me that dragonflies alighted on me when I swam where there was frogbit, greater reedmace, water forget-me-not, the yellow fists of waterlilies, *nuphar lutea*, and the dazzling blue arched backs of mating damselflies. I had the company of a heron perched in an ash tree. It was more than pleasant to write in the shade.

But, as the weeks passed, I began to realize that a curious inertia was developing in the garden, and then a distinct unease. Birds stopped singing. Grasshoppers seemed reluctant to jump. Fruit stopped swelling. At night there was the frequent winking of lightning beyond the horizon accompanied by distant thunder, but the sky could not break down and weep, and there was no drizzle. There was only sterile thunder and no rain. When the Perseid showers came in August, the north-eastern sky was scribbled on but hatched no generous ignitions. Meteors made only trivial arcs and suffered brief extinctions. There was no shortage of unprovoked wasp and bee stings, suggesting bad tempers. The mulberry tree, its gnarled elbows on the ground, was full of bloody murders and rotted berries. Sunflowers let their heads loll forward, lacking the will to look up, and many plants and crops lost their appetite for growth. Tired grass and exhausted yarrow were baked brown. Glow-worms failed to light. There was a bruised sky. Nowhere was there any purpose or any remaining rumbustiousness. It was a strange time of waiting – not only for the rain to come or the crash of thundersnow, but for the end of something indefinable and unknown.

Meanwhile, the latest wave of infection began to work itself out. No measures could halt it. By now doctors and nurses were exhausted, ill or dead. It was worse than the last time. Italy, Spain, Germany, Greece, Turkey, the Balkan region and Russia had record numbers of cases. Health services everywhere were on the point of collapse. Hospitals were unable to cope and, instead, people were treated in parked cars.

It became impossible to enforce lockdowns. Armies and police struggled against rioting, maskless crowds in many cities, especially Paris, Leipzig and Naples. In Liège, doctors were told to continue working while infected, infecting their patients. Students who had returned to English universities infected each other at a rate even higher than in the civilian population outside and, refusing to be locked in, broke out to spread the plague.

Migrants in West Africa and the Sahel, unable to cross land borders closed by the pandemic, drowned trying to reach Europe by sea, mostly off the coast of Libya. In Switzerland, doctors asked people over sixty to sign Do Not Resuscitate orders because all intensive care units and hospitals were full, and Geneva had the highest infection rate in Europe. A state of emergency was declared in Australia and people were forbidden to go outside.

There were still politicians who, despite the carnage, refused to take the virus seriously. Mexico, without testing, Brazil, Argentina and India had the highest death tolls apart from America, where the unhinged and despotic president discharged himself from hospital, lost an election but refused to leave office, obstructing quarantine arrangements. He went about shouting 'I won! I won!' while deaths increased exponentially, many people falling ill for a second time. New cases tripled in a month and millions of Americans, anticipating some dreadful showdown, bought guns. Economies were wrecked. Money was rapidly printed and distributed to countless unemployed.

Daumier on not Finishing

On not finishing. Some paintings break off as if they have said as much as they need to say but are averse to the idea of completion. Better just to end. Like the person who does not say goodbye, but instead exits untainted by valediction. Of course they could finish but they choose simply to stop, and only afterwards do you come to realize that the transitory was in fact the terminus, the passage the limit, the process the finale. Little did you know it was the last time. But people's last words tend to stick in the mind, and it is exactly the same with paintings.

What Daumier really likes in the way of literature is *Don Quixote*. He keeps it by his bed and rereads it constantly. What is it about Cervantes's tremendous knockabout confusion of fact and fiction that has a direct bearing on Daumier's view of the world? Don Quixote, in changing his name, hunting up his great-great-grandfather's mouldy armour and rechristening his old horse, chooses to become prey to his delusions because they please him. People he encounters, seeing that he is off his head, humour and mock him but, because he thinks everything he has read in chivalric history is true, he preserves his dignity. He combines the admirable with the futile. After all, he is entirely ill-suited to his agreeable role. His age and physique should alone disqualify him, but his withered and dusty visage, courteous demeanour and grave voice equip him wonderfully to wander through the four quarters of the world in quest of adventures; just as Sancho Panza, riding upon his ass like any patriarch, vehemently desires to be governor of the island Don Quixote has promised him as his reward, 'be it never so big'. And in the final three pages, after their countless bruising tussles with real life, Don Quixote comes to himself and dies entirely sane.

Daumier as caricaturist spends every day, and meets every deadline, drawing the risible encounters between reality and fiction, between the anti-heroic plebian and the heroic idealistic. When he has a moment to himself and can paint unsolicited, he does not so much illustrate *Don Quixote* as reflect on his version of the world. He does not need to show the pasteboard visor or provide information about sheep and windmills, but only the true and solid protagonists with their brown shadows quickly drawn in oil paint. Poor Rosinante needs only to be given bones sticking out like the corners of a *real*, a sharp-sided coin, and the knight's head need be no more than the knob on a banister, for a land to be evoked full of combats, challenges, wounds, courtships and amours. When Don Quixote sits to read, an old man intent on his heavy book, may he not be Daumier himself?

Now think of the Île Saint-Louis, in Paris, where Daumier lives and works for many years after his marriage to 'Didine', a dressmaker, in 1846. The island lies like a fish in the river, its head to the east end of Notre-Dame. Rue Saint-Louis-en-l'Île is the island's spine. Wander down this, turn north up the narrow bone of rue Poulletier and look up at Daumier's attic window in the tall old row that is number 9 Quai d'Anjou. Tied up next to you are laundry barges, the same as on Quai de Montebello, chains of smoke going up from their iron chimneys, and a row of *badauds*, unemployed onlookers, sits on the low wall, two of them fishing. It is a working-class area, scarred by historical events, partly grey, the grey of the pavé, and partly the sepia colour of cuttlefish ink. Baudelaire lives nearby, in the much grander house that is number 17 Hôtel Pimodan, and has felt the bat-wing of madness, as he describes it, brush his head as he goes in at his door. The poet Gautier also. And, because it is cheap, the island has long been the home of Gautier's brilliant collaborator Gérard de Nerval, who wears two shirts against the cold and whose distressed moon-face, haunted by insane asylums, Daumier sometimes encounters on

Quai d'Orléans. In January 1855, Nerval crosses the river, goes down the dark steps behind rue de la Vielle Lanterne and hangs himself successfully, the last of his several attempts at suicide. It is possible to see exactly what all these people look like at the time in the photographs, unadorned as police mug-shots, taken by Nadar.

Daumier looks tired. Although famous for his countless caricatures in *Le Charivari* and for his lithographs, he is permanently broke. Twice he has been to prison for political cartoons and twice been fined. For his paintings, which he almost never shows or sells, he is not known at all except by a handful of other artists. There are no laugh lines round his eyes, although in his drawings of human behaviour he can be incomparably funny. Though a lion on behalf of the poor and downtrodden when he has a pencil in his hand, he is shy. A quiet, modest man, who is beginning to worry about his eyesight.

He stands for a long moment at the gap in the wall opposite his door where the wet flight of steps leads down to the river. A young woman with a small child and a bundle of laundry comes heavily up the steps and pushes past him. On the far side of the river, to the north, the tall roofs and attics are yellowish, like an irregular cliff in weak sunlight.

Dulcinea did not know she was Dulcinea. Without even noticing him, a girl in the next village becomes the subject of Don Quixote's devoted attention. This girl with the laundry, whom Daumier sees most days, becomes the unknowing subject of six or seven paintings. He does not use models. He does not draw her directly. He paints her bulk and her action as best he can from memory, including the steps, the river and the far bank. It is her labour he paints, her rounded shoulders and bulky shadow, and from that flows his comment on poverty and exhaustion. He sees the same exhaustion in the frantic saltimbanque with no audience, the worn-out wrestler, the terrified litigant in court, the deaf woman in the corner of a third-class railway carriage. His brush goes round the form, because he is a caricaturist, with much the same speed that his crayon greases a lithographic stone, but the result, though pithy, has a sober depth. Now, it says, in oil paint I am serious.

I deeply mind about these people because I am one of them. A lifelong Republican. I may not draw them correctly but I convey to you the truth of their burden and the weight of the injustice they suffer. Here is the brown space in which they live. Sometimes it is empty. I will put in the emptiness too, the uncompanionable gap between one thing and another, one person and another, in quickly drawn paint.

Behind him he can sense Millet. And when Van Gogh sees what Daumier is doing, he stops a drawing he is making of a woman pulling carrots in the snow and dashes off a letter to Theo. 'I want,' he writes, 'to learn to make those very incorrectnesses, deviations, remodellings, changes of reality, so that they may become untruth but *more* true than the literal truth.' In another place he observes that, when Daumier paints a figure, 'the shape will be felt much more. And yet the proportions may be almost arbitrary, the anatomy and structure wrong, but it will LIVE.'

Suffice it to say that Daumier, like a saltimbanque, deals in tempo, backflip and stillness. His brushing in the paintings makes shapes like a long line of refugees or a heavy tarpaulin blown in the wind. At other times, it suddenly reverses a dark shape into a light one and within the shadow there are the round knobs of skulls, like his clay heads, their pates and jaws showing that human beings are here without the need of detail. And, third, there is that absolute stillness, made by shadow, when a man stands silently examining a portfolio in bad light, or Don Quixote reads his book, a joke falls flat or an artist contemplates his canvas, alone. All these wonderful and inexplicable pictures have tremendous grandeur of conception and a simple dribbling bareness of paint.

Eventually Daumier leaves his attic on the Île Saint-Louis, lives for a time in boulevard de Clichy and then moves to a tiny house to the north-west of Paris, at Valmondois. He finds it difficult to see. When he can no longer afford to pay his rent, his old friend Corot secretly buys the house at Valmondois and gives it to Daumier without him knowing it. Both men are offered the Légion d'honneur and both refuse it. Finally, his artist friends arrange an exhibition of Daumier's work in Paris, at Durand-Ruel's gallery, which includes ninety-four oil paintings. The exhibition is a failure and less than a year later Daumier dies of a heart attack in the garden behind his house at Valmondois.

The whole business of not finishing, because Don Quixote dies sane, now becomes a question of[1]

I shut out the world's grief and would not listen to it. In the
garden there was confused heat. Peppery colours. Something
was averse to time. Instead there appeared some gigantic
loftiness, a magniloquence, as if the process of the natural world
far transcended the plague, outdwarfing all that was human. But
I could not read it yet.

Perhaps, to some appalling theology, endeavour might
be a solution. Chaos was out of sight beyond the scorched
landscape. And so, with vehemence, I tried the crude resort
of labour.

For weeks I could not write, but I could water, weed and
harvest. It occurred to me that instead of manhandling words
into order I should use this time to grow useful vegetables
and bake bread. Now I could reconcile myself to the situation,
without feigning, by an intermission of steep labour. This might
drive all sadness with a vengeance past death to a pledge of
immortality.

Fruit trees I had planted forty years before were now bearing
luxuriantly. In the orchard, with the pleasantness of tall,
tapering wooden ladders, apple boxes, hurdles and barrows,
I picked red apples against the blue sky for a month. There
were the three hottest consecutive September days since 1929.
There was plum picking, damson picking, pear picking. High
canopies, the warm aromas of wood and fruit. In the distance
a yaffle laughed. The old jokes are the best. Round me was the
question of pointlessness and the dance of late butterflies.
There were meadow browns, painted ladies, peacocks, orange
commas. I picked and wheeled away the misshapen but
delicious apples called Catsheads, first mentioned in 1629.
The early monastic apple, Coeur de Boeuf. Broad-eyed pippins.
Ribston pippins, 1707, and Worcester pearmains, 1873. Where
was the truth to be found?

Because there was still no rain I spent early mornings and late evenings watering. Lipstick-red gladioli, rudbeckias, dahlias, heleniums, agapanthus, sweet peas, chrome-yellow bearded irises. And exhausted vegetables. Runner beans, marrows and pumpkins. The temperature remained in the nineties. There were garden warblers in the raspberries, Vs of geese high up. Small frogs. Goldfinches. Morning glories, pale blue. Glittering night skies. Bats in my bedroom. Pipistrelles. Noisy owls.

But I could not understand what, if anything, the garden seemed so intent on telling me. And, in the landscape, strong flour and yeast had been swollen by the plague into something unrecognizable. An unfamiliar sublimity. Nature was magnificently various and strange but, for all that, I was pitifully unable to decipher its hieroglyphics. I could not read it, and the pilgrimage of my mind itself became an unknown region.

Rouault

The old head is propped on a pillow. Someone has put a crucifix on his chest. Another crucifix is on the wall beside the bed. He wears the round white hat he often wore for printing, the paper hat of a dumbstruck clown. He looks exhausted.

He thinks: I lie at a margin beyond which no man can see. But who have I been for eighty-six years, for all this time? So much still to be completed. The melancholy of the incomplete coincides with no certainties. I will not sleep easy in the dust. I join all that is ramshackle and tossed away. A cruel God to destroy the beauty of the song. My work interrupted, marked 'Unfinished due to Death'. The mystery upon the street is that the visible exists. Drains away the dancing mind. The panic-stricken skeleton cocks a bone ear. That is the sound of the senses wagging their wings to flee. Who partitioned me from me? I know that colour corresponds inexplicably to changes of mood, that there is intuition beyond reason and that everything is plainly audible to the addict of memory. I know that sanctity is clean ground to me. Short-lived the singing proved. Today I become the crony of the brown dead.

February 12th, 1958. Georges Rouault has a long night and a morning remaining. Like Christ mocked, he tries to go through them methodically. He turns his head. He thinks: I recognize the foetid farrago with scythe and frown as my own inventions, and I recognize the cough. Death, you play *my* part. I saw that the people were in hell, that even the hermits who died kneeling could no longer inspire them to raptures of divine love, so I put my feelings into paintings and prints. The ideas I wished to communicate, not

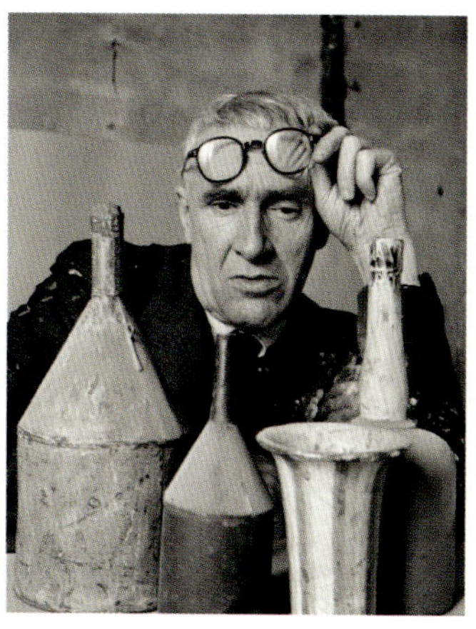

17 Giorgio Morandi photographed by Herbert List, 1953.

18 Giorgio Morandi, *Still Life*, 1963, oil on canvas.

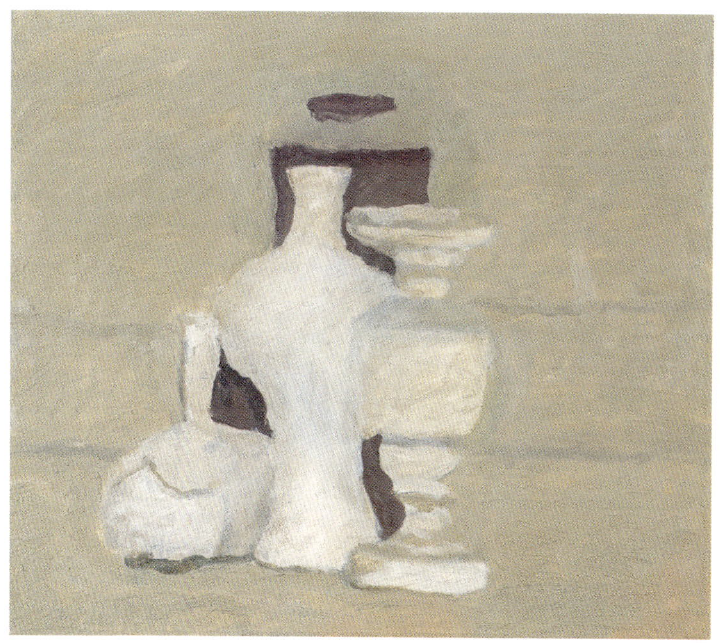

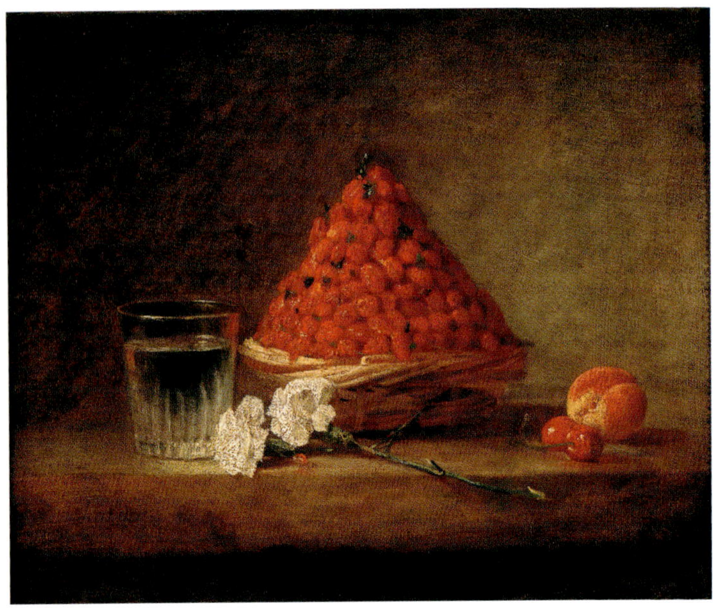

19 Jean-Baptiste-Siméon Chardin, *Basket with Wild Strawberries*, c. 1760–61, oil on canvas.

20 Jean-Baptiste-Siméon Chardin, *Self-Portrait with Eye-shade*, 1775, pastel on paper.

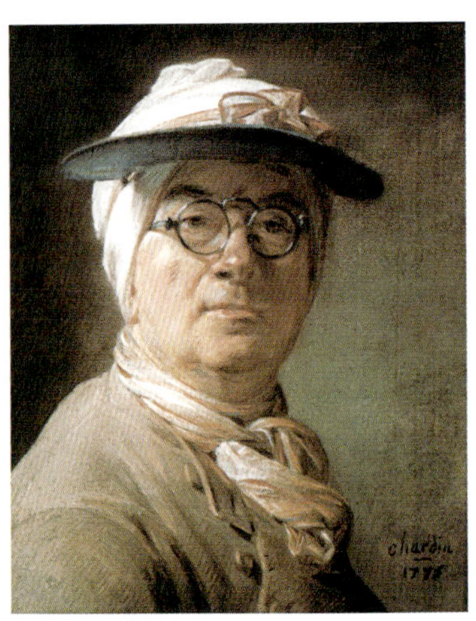

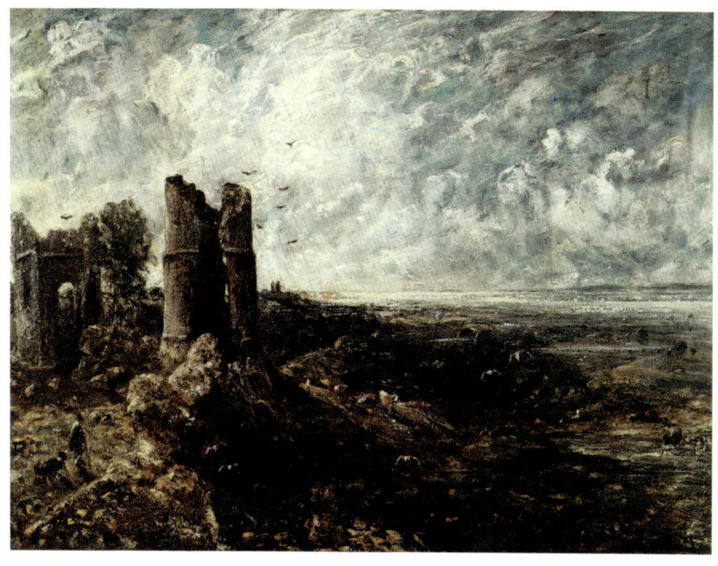

21 John Constable, *Sketch for 'Hadleigh Castle'*, *c.* 1828–29, oil on canvas.

22 John Constable, *A Cottage at East Bergholt*, 1830s, oil on canvas.

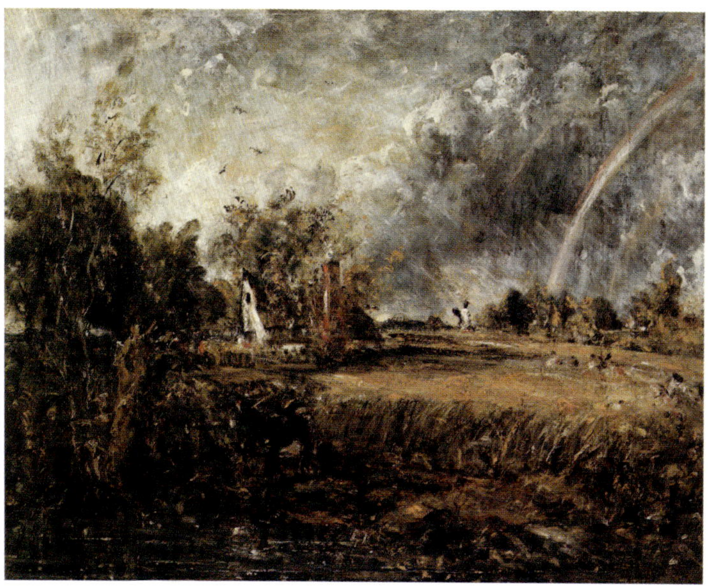

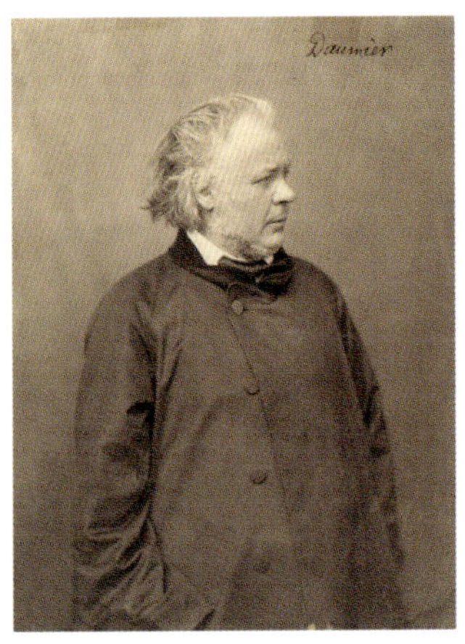

23 Honoré Daumier, photographed by Nadar, *c.* 1857.

24 Honoré Daumier, *Don Quixote*, *c.* 1868, oil on canvas.

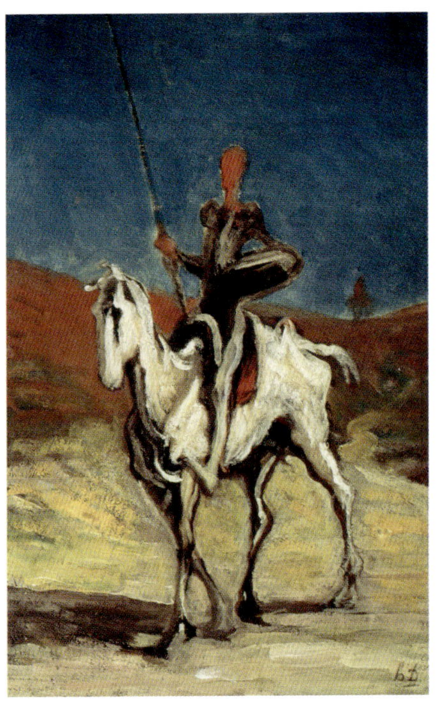

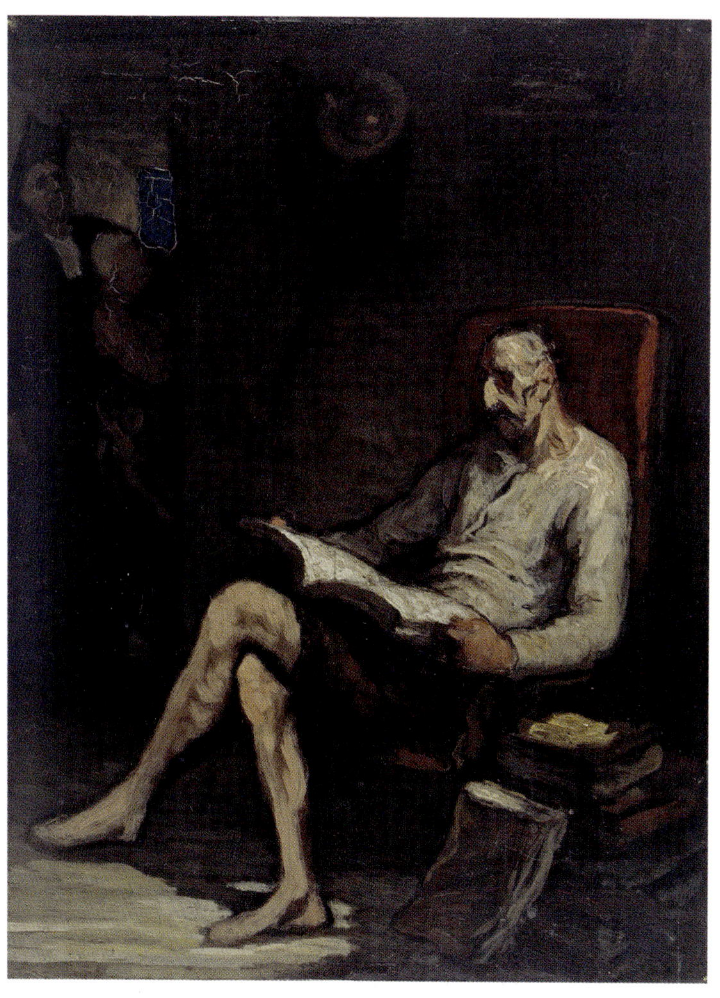

25 Honoré Daumier, *Don Quixote Reading, c.* 1867, oil on wood panel.

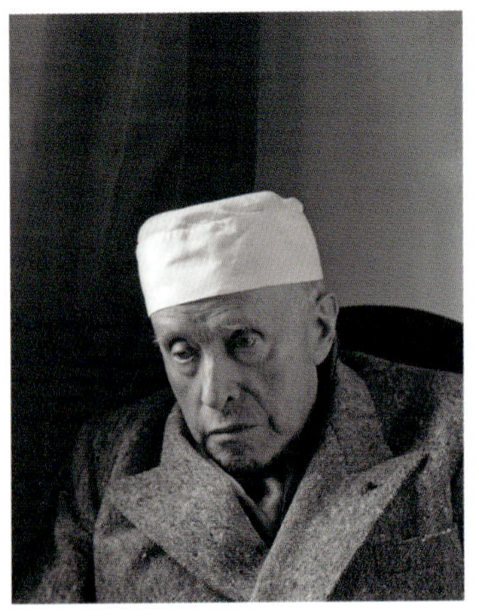

26 Georges Rouault photographed by
Arnold Newman (detail), 1957.

27 Georges Rouault, *Crucifixion*, 1939,
oil on paper.

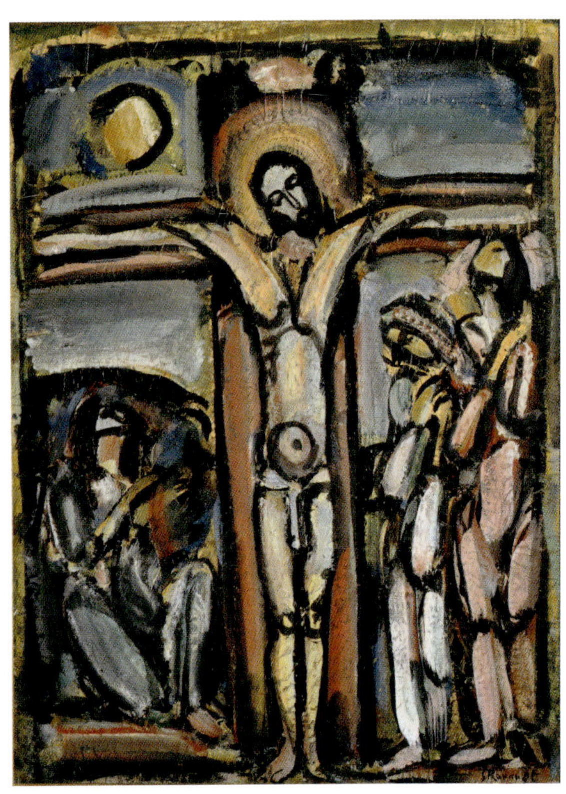

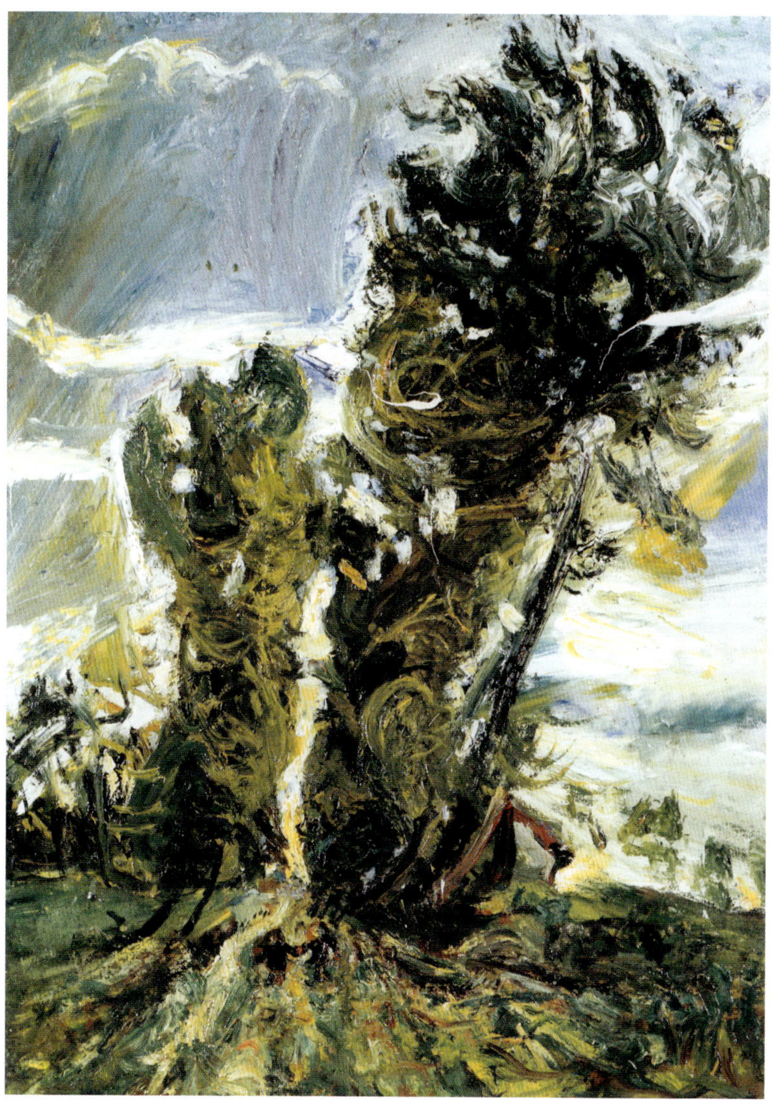

28 Chaïm Soutine, *Large Poplars at Civry or: After the Storm*, *c.* 1939–40, oil on canvas.

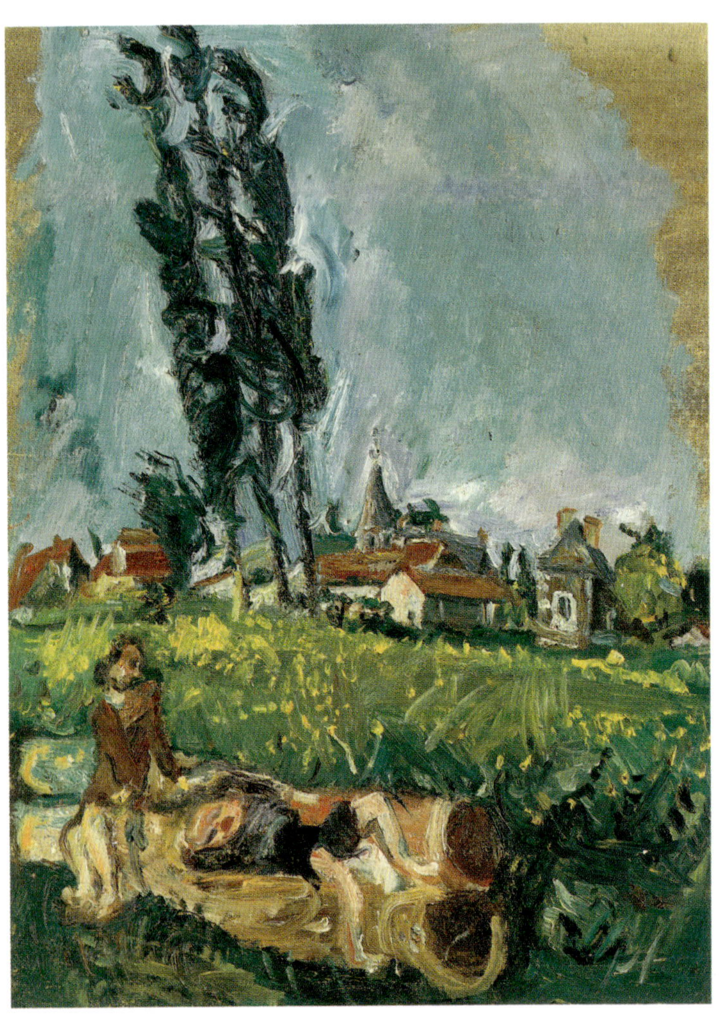

29 Chaïm Soutine, *Children Playing at Champigny*,
c. 1942–43, oil on canvas.

being facts, would not go into language, and the only things that exist do so beyond words. The misuse of words is serious, and religious utterances are unverifiable. While Rouault thought this, a drunk in the street below blew a long phrase on a preposition and Rouault smiled, or would have smiled had he not been weeping. Archaeologists, he remembered, had for years been excavating wasted tears.

Lying on top of the bed, not in it, he thinks of Belleville, the racy and anarchic north Parisian suburb in which he grew up, and of all the characters there. Of their poverty. Of how his father, the cabinet-maker, lived simply. Of how he, Rouault, drew on his mother's father's floor in the Marais, and of the smells and sounds when, as a boy, he discovered the book-boîtes on the quays of the Seine and first saw the reproductions they sold, slightly damp, of prints after Daumier and Courbet, so dark and complete in their compositions. And the barges had their cumbersome reasons. He took to drawing them in the very early mornings, the bargees already with their shirts off in summer, loading. He thought of the circus that came to Belleville, the clowns and strongmen, wrestlers, bareback riders. Paris. Paris as a great parade of the poor and suffering, as a microcosm of the whole suffering world. The butchers and the elderly girls of the street. Those condemned to entertain.

It had been in many ways an ideal childhood, even with the cheats and narks, the deluded, the foul-mouthed, the aggressive, the minor officials, the humourists, the usurers. Even the story they liked to tell of his own birth: how Paris was under bombardment by government troops in 1871 at the time of the Commune and how, on the last day of the year, a shell struck the side of their house as his mother began her labour and they carried her down to the cellar, where he was born. It was an old joke that, when his terrified father arrived home expecting to find the whole family dead, the concierge told him, 'Not at all. There's one more since you went out.'

Lying there, he feels the cold stain him. He imagines three black cliffs with reflections the colour of jet and sloe that put him in mind of oblivion. But then, quite suddenly, he is reminded of the resplendent blues, reds and greens that he saw during his apprenticeship in the workshop of the stained-glass maker. Minds change colour. Dreamers make discoveries with the clarity of hindsight. Black lines curve round a yellow sea. Then he thought of his dear master, Gustave Moreau, at the École des Beaux-Arts. Moreau, the childhood neighbour of Delacroix, whose passion for colour and richly compounded texture led Rouault to become Moreau's favourite pupil. Moreau, small of stature, would flare up. What he was looking for was a convinced painter of sacred art. Curtains opened on an inward landscape. Rouault at eighteen, with all his passion for the old masters and all his skill at drawing, being encouraged by Moreau to go beyond them into his own world, to follow his expressive instincts, to paint faster and more freely, to find some way out of the sententious and the ox-like to the immediacy of first-hand experience, using all Paris as his urgent topic. What a heartbreaking attempt it had been. 'You will be alone', Moreau warned him, shortly before he died, leaving both him and Matisse bereft of their old teacher and perfect exemplar, but he meant it proudly. Moreau always knew what Rouault needed. He needed to breathe unpolluted air and be true to himself. To know the joys, though almost overwhelmed by the difficulties because everything had to be paid for. Just work for yourself, Moreau told him.

And that was when, living in Montmartre, Rouault had the elation of the furious experiment in rue Rochechouart. Oh, how he had wanted life then, to draw in the key of Cézanne's blue and make perfect sense without ever being understood. He could not afford oil paint, but that was of no consequence because on paper there was ink, watercolour, gouache, spit, pencil, all appropriate to a rapid, nervous, explosive and marvellously anxious way of drawing, of which the subject became human frailty.

Now he twitches and would, if he could, kick his numb legs in the air because he can remember all too well how, by a simple device, he was able to draw that long series of women. He and a few friends, unable to afford a model, decided they would join together to hire a cheap room in rue Rochechouart, with a stove in it. Then they let it be known that the street women of Montmartre were free to come in if they needed to warm themselves. This was in 1905. For years he had a supply of magnificent models, whose plight and flesh he drew with sympathy. Many of them were heavy, worn out. You can see in the drawings what it is to be young and then no longer young, to be well and then no longer well. The sitters are, many of them, cut off from being the people they were. Rouault drew them quickly, with a maximum of smudging, scratching and fierce expression. Though sometimes half in disguise as odalisques reclining, they reveal themselves as garrulous, heartbroken, puny, mountainous, condemned. So much unloved acreage of skin and limb. His drawings of them offended his Catholic friends, and he lost the support, most painfully, of his spiritual mentor Léon Bloy. But he realized now, perhaps courtesy of Daumier and Goya, that this violent means of drawing character would extend with authenticity into the rest of his cast, the travelling circus of human frailty and cruelty that he saw to be always around him. If he could draw with sympathy he could draw also with contempt. Now he was rough and unbiddable as well as solitary.

Rouault, on the bed, begins to flex his bone hands as if they would lay hold of collars. Collars of the pretentious, the minor official puffed up, the pedant, the fanatic, the landlord, fops, quacks, lawyers, judges. This long parade he drew with scorn, as if appalled, while the media accumulated. But then he began to see that sometimes these different categories overlapped in a disconcerting way, that there was somehow less difference than he had supposed between accuser and accused, between judges and judged, and that in the earth and dried blood of this human texture all men are prisoners, trapped, enslaved.

Enslaved. Rouault lies back, no longer drumming. I was enslaved, he thinks, by Ambroise Vollard. For twelve years. I feel exhausted at the very thought of it. And yet it was from this that my real and lasting work emerged. It is true that, from 1917 until 1930, Rouault was more or less adopted by the dealer Vollard, who not only bought his entire output of drawings and paintings but commissioned him on an unimaginably grand scale to make prints. Vollard, the formidable champion of Cézanne and Gauguin, was by this time a private dealer and publisher of *éditions de luxe* which would come to include Picasso's *Vollard Suite*. Rouault, by nature an inveterate worker, was provided by Vollard with a studio at 28 rue de Martignac, and there, in human bondage, he deliberately set himself to live extremely simply and to work and work at prints.

Why? Because he realized that into the ponderous business of printmaking could pass his torrent of Parisian characters, who would emerge, not as casualties damaged by life, but as monumental statements of high seriousness, as aphorisms, as images so grand and beautiful and of such authority that they could stand with an air of finality. And then become oil paintings.

Majestically, the resounding twenty years of later work in oil paint began. The retired prostitutes reappeared most regally, and the clowns, so pitied, became the tormented Christ. The little landscapes Rouault had always painted, based on the Île-de-France and the Seine-et-Marne, became the radiant settings for the flight into Egypt, and his beloved working-class Belleville, without effort, became Jerusalem. The turbulence of mixed media on paper slowed down and transformed with tremendous solemnity into the structure of glazed and layered oil paint. It accrued over the years. It was in his nature to keep his pictures constantly around him and to work at them periodically, long after the initial event. The fortunate sense of nuance, he said, came gradually through steadfast labour. Nothing seemed to him to be finished, so nothing must leave the studio. The fifty-eight plates of the *Miserere*, many of which went through at least twelve states, were published at last thirty years after they were begun. As if this monumental effort were not enough, there were two other print series as well: *Les Reincarnations du Père Ubu* (1918–21) and *Les Fleurs du mal* (1926–27). The blackness and reworked shades of pain in all of these provided the mighty source and engine of all his subjects, which are all parts of the same great cry of suffering.

And then you begin to see in the paintings, as this cry is repeated over and over again like reiterated prayer or the litany of the church, that all this points to a conclusion. As the colour swells and ripens and the halo of light increases, there is the agonized realization that, beyond role-playing and beyond war, greed, pride, hypocrisy, hats, uniforms, medals and viciousness, there is the possibility of redemption. They are all bearers of misery and inflictors of pain, these people: the bourgeoisie in masks of pomposity, the society women confident of their seats booked in the afterlife, the poor, the sad-faced clowns who are doubles of Rouault, the prodigal sons, the refugees, the suffering Christ so often painted, scraped down, repainted, damaged, wounded and remade in ever richer and more leathery pigment, are far more than who they are. *Miserere mei, Deus, secundum magnam misericordiam tuam.* Have mercy upon me, O God, according to thy loving kindness. They are the key to salvation.

Rouault went nowhere and accepted no honours. He continued to work. 'For this poor devil,' he said, 'art is his only reason for being. One does not enter tradition as one would a bus.'

Now he presses his jaw down into his chest, the better to see the window at the foot of the bed. Outside is the corner of a building and a triangle of lit sky. Could he but lift his head he would howl for wasted time. He longs to see contentment between buildings, a gentler order of feeling, public monuments to lack of pain, squares laid out for peace of mind. Painting, he thinks, is virgin territory still. My head is a capital which empties in summer. I am absent from rigmarole. Outside, below the window, Paris. '*Paris mon pays,*' he whispers. '*Paris mon pays.* The broad road taken by us all towards a lost eternity. I hope to see all these things again in paradise. The colour. The light. Most of all, the light. In the enormous dawn, I'll see that the blank of the page which intervenes is a moment known to me.'

*Elation at the advent of a vaccine was mixed with concern at the
news that at least two new versions of the virus had been present
in the population of England for months and had been spreading,
undetected, much more rapidly than the first. The new strains
caused pandemonium. People were asked not to leave London
in a forlorn attempt to curb the spread but there was widespread
civil disobedience. Crowded trains of infected people travelled to all
parts of the country. European borders and ports were closed. Many
countries banned British visitors. Trade became almost impossible
so that the London Stock Exchange was close to collapse and
the government considered imposing a universal lockdown. The
intention was that all should be isolated in their homes and no one
should go out.*

*People were now seriously frightened. The exhausted National
Health Service was on the point of being completely overwhelmed
and, by the winter solstice, it looked as if the plague in Britain was
out of control.*

And at the solstice, in a clear sky, Saturn and Jupiter came so
close together that they appeared as a single bright object, a
phenomenon not seen since 1623. The planets approached their
conjunction when they were close to the narrow sliver of new
moon in the southern sky. A comet, in a graceful arc, made its
way between planets and moon.

The garden seemed to die, though catkins were an inch long
and buds shiny on the wych elm. Fieldfare conversations whirred
past to invisible roosts, which sounded sizeable, in tall trees.
Scarlet bryony vines draped hedges. The winter heliotrope was
flowering, and Italian arums started to exhibit their leaves with
showy white veins. Clusters of ivy berries were purple-black.
There was ice under pollarded willows.

When daylight lost heart by early afternoon, I retreated
indoors. In summer the rooms had smelled of flowers but

now they smelled of books and woodsmoke. They were full of pictures. It was no hardship to work at my table all day with a big fire burning, the garden locked in icy semi-darkness outside, and a Rouault to look at.

It is a very old house, Tudor, and mostly semi-derelict, though that did not seem to matter very much now. There had been times when it was well run and full of cheerful children and many dogs, and times when it had been almost empty, and now it was all but empty again. Its old rooms were still beautiful, consoling and humane. I liked the library, which had mostly books about painting, philosophy and poetry. There was an office with books on architecture and gardening. There was a freezing bedroom with a ceiling that went up to the apex of the roof, and another old bedroom with an arch in it that had mostly watercolours. There were many beautiful paintings, etchings by Goya and Cézanne, and no shortage of drawings. Now that everything was coming to an end, I knew that I had never been happier anywhere than I was here, though I was beginning to hurt.

Soutine

At Civry-sur-Serein, in the department of Yonne, near Auxerre. Summer 1939. Chaïm Soutine is painting the avenue of tall aspens which lines the road to the village of L'Isle-sur-Serein. He has a black forelock and a cigarette. He is forty-seven. Height five foot two inches. Heavy face, abnormally small white hands with little fingers that he holds out in front of him when he walks. Speaks French with a thick Russian accent. He has rather a slobbering way of speaking, but not exactly a speech impediment. He does not wash very much. His character is extremely volatile. He is in pain. He has stomach ulcers.

The blue trees do not quite meet overhead. It has taken him ten visits to find these particular trees. There have been times recently when he has gone weeks on end without painting because of the pain and also because of a certain lassitude, but now he returns to paint them every day. He does not begin painting at once but regards them for a long time, perhaps twenty minutes, before beginning to paint. He does not draw them first. There are no drawings by Soutine. When he at last begins, he maps in the trees' relative positions in deep paint, almost in a frenzy. The clumsiness and disorder that characterize him in everyday life are replaced by an extreme ardour and almost violent athleticism. He works impulsively, in high excitement and at speed. He knows from experience to keep the paint clean, so he throws aside, jettisons, clogged brushes. No time to clear them. If the gesturing in the paint begins to lose resonance he ups the key, resorting to slashes of red for emphasis or deep blue for legibility. Very often he takes advantage of the fact that his brushes carry two or more colours at the same time, enabling him to draw with them simultaneously. He is quick to capitalize on fortunate accidents, drips, runs, spatters, which add to the animation of the scribbled surface. But nothing is arbitrary. Everything, everything derives most scrupulously from what he can see in front of him.

Consider these trees. At one moment the clouds part and a vertical streak of bright light breaks through the roof of the avenue. He transposes it with a large, single, violent brushstroke. Among the foliage the breeze makes what amounts to a tidal rip which convulses it first to one side then the other. One rapid piece of drawing is destroyed and immediately overturned by another on the off chance of further progress. The vibrating and quivering of the leaves incite Soutine to turbulent sequences of drawing in wet paint. He appears to breathe in sympathy with the trees' dimensions. One instant they are all air. They both cancel and admit the sky. Their great height dominates and exhilarates him. Far above him they rattle their temporary shade.

The trees are on a bend. Occasionally a man with a cart or a man leading a calf will appear round the corner, or a couple of the local children running, and he will dash them in, more for scale than for anything else, only to brush them out later. Often in the pictures you can make out the scars of absent figures or animals on roads or paths. They are prone across them, only their shadows remaining rather than the upright form, a mule on its side in the mud. And then after three hours, he breaks off and for a further three hours he is reluctant to speak, from exhaustion.

Finishing a painting saddens him. The result, in a curious way, becomes of little interest to him. You must understand that what he wants is not so much the painting as the process. He would never hang a picture or show it. In fact he is more than likely to destroy it with much the same violence with which it was made in the first place. People, like his patrons Monsieur and Madame Castaing, soon learn that if they want a picture by Soutine they have to hide it from him, or buy it and take it away before he can cut it up or paint over it.

Medicine seems to him to be in its infancy and his guts are an enigma to him. He is many different people, divided, unknown to himself, elusive and always in great disquiet. In a way, he is seeking to remake the world, and his painting is a religion which is merciless. He lives in a foreign land and is solitary. He has moved furiously about, backwards and forwards, trying to find and destroy much of his earlier output because he has turned against it and come to think of it as worthless.

What you are seeing, when Soutine paints the Auxerre trees, is what I think happens in the work of most of the artists I have written about here. This storm of temperament is true painting, an inexplicable combination of seeing, feeling, memory, response, imagination and profound oddness. And so he turns away in exhaustion.

In three years' time, during the slow and circuitous train journey to Paris, where he will die in agony, Soutine will think of these trees again.

Do not look for explanations. Painting as profound as this will not be explained. But there are two things you could notice.

Soutine was born the tenth of eleven children in a Lithuanian village in Western Russia in 1893. The place, Smilavičy, was a collection of broken-down grey huts which housed about 400 people, not far from Minsk. His father was a poor mender. His mother showed him no affection and he was half starved. But the defining characteristic of shtetl life was its violent expression of emotion, the constant hubbub of noise, anger, passion, argument. This outpouring of feelings, the rapid and volatile emotional response, zest, were the essential currency of daily life.

And, second, there was the shibboleth that surrounded looking. The whole business of scrutiny and the evil eye. Looking was in effect something to be kept to a minimum. Its implications were sinful. Drawing and painting were prohibited because of this and partly because, in a bitterly poor family, they were commercially worthless. Soutine was beaten because he showed an interest in them, and his eventual escape from Smilavičy came about as a direct result of it. When he was sixteen he asked a pious Jew in the shtetl, a rabbi, to sit for him for a portrait and was so badly beaten up by the man's family that he eventually received a small sum in compensation for his injuries. He used this to go to Minsk for art lessons, and a year later he succeeded at his second attempt in entering the art school at Vilnius. Here, for the first time, he saw old master paintings in reproduction. And, eventually, his obsession got him by train to Paris.

Still, the passion for looking. Still the starvation. He cadged in cafés, worked in railway stations and as a ditch digger. In the Louvre in 1919–20 you could very often have seen the awkward, ill-looking Soutine hanging around for whole days in front of Courbet's *Burial at Ornans*. He was besotted with it and with the Rembrandts, much as Proust was obsessed with Vermeer's *View of Delft*, watching for the cloud shadow to move across the town, and as Cézanne had stood for hours at a time in front of pictures by Poussin.

And so began Soutine's art of urgent psychological necessity, a kind of nervous pandemonium which depended on passionate scrutiny. The still lifes in which the dead world is alive and the elastic idea is always in motion. Soutine sets out in his art to violate everything he was ever taught in the shtetl about shibboleths to do with meat. Not only does he stare, he, who is hungry, violates all kosher rules which require animals to be killed quickly and with the minimum of blood. Cadavers stretch. A fowl hangs by its beak. Everything is painted in fat, blood, lard and spittle. Tables are cut down to strand fish. The tines of forks become the ribcage of a dog. As paint becomes flesh and flesh paint, there approaches almost a bloodbath of the most beautiful passages of scarlet and green. Even gladioli struggle in scarlet petals against brown. There develops a convulsive appetite for tabletops with utensils, vegetables and slaughtered meat. Just off the beat, swung away from the obvious phrase, cut and slit this way and that, are the most astonishing asymmetric designs, so daring that they are probably cut down. Spittle is mahogany, spittle a violin, spittle Courbet's trout.

The portraits too. He does not really know these people, or very few of them. Madeleine Castaing, whom he knew very well because she tried to rescue him, is painted with the same depth of psychology (*Portrait of Madeleine Castaing*, c. 1929, Metropolitan Museum of Art, New York) as the *Woman in Pink* (c. 1924, Saint Louis Art Museum), whose wonderfully racked face is coiled into the coiled arms and hands of her plush chair, or the superb *Woman in Red* with the enormous hat of *c.* 1924 (Private collection). The pictures are a way of exaggerating people in paint. Many of them are in uniform. Uniforms provoke posing. A cavalcade of characters is crucified on chairs. Sometimes sitters hang their bones over the backs of chairs like jackets. They have all-but-detached puppet arms and legs, and meaty hands. And, as paint becomes matter, up through the dashes of oil, like surfacing fish, come people with wet eyes and personalities and opinions.

Soutine fastens onto the peculiarities, oddnesses, quirks that poke through the adopted logos of dressing up. The put-upon, the weaselly, the humorous. Some bring their egos with them, even a degree of sophistication in the form of a stylish hat set carefully down on a chair beside them. Among the hotel staff especially there is a bit of dash. The hands on the knees. The hotel manager is *all* uniform. There is the insolent bellhop, the obstreperous waiter, the valet with a face as red as his waistcoat, the pastry cook wrapped like a pig in white, the head waiter all carmine angularity, those who are bullying, obnoxious, arrogant. Those who, including the children and the room-service boy between shifts, cannot wait to get away. Those, well turned out, raffish, who actually want to be painted, and those who are distinctly self-conscious, look sideways and would rather be somewhere else. There is the butcher's boy who appears to be painted in blood. Later come the women, most of whom are candidates for walk-on parts in 1930s novels. He painted them while repeatedly rubbing his face, red as a turkey, his eyes wide, muttering. The English reader, the Swiss girl, the lady in the cloche hat, the neurotic, the woman with a green bead necklace, the maids with hands like frightened animals in their laps, the Jewish woman in the salon. All of them shot through with green veins. What is life but anxiety, pretension, clothes, paint and meat?

Soutine worked in the curious circular system of studios called La Ruche, in Montparnasse, where he met Chagall, and tried unsuccessfully to keep the bugs out of his ears in the communal house infested with vermin at the Cité Falguière. He begged and borrowed money. From where he tried to sleep he could hear the railway sidings and the outlandish noise of the slaughterhouse at Vaugirard. Then his Polish dealer, Zborowski, to whom he had been introduced by Modigliani, suggested he try to paint outside Paris. He went on a brief trip in 1918 to Vence and Cagnes-sur-Mer, where the red steps are. Then Zborowski gave him a small allowance with which to buy paints, and just enough food to keep him alive, and sent him off in 1919 to Céret, a small town at the eastern end of the Pyrenees.

Céret. Céret. Like many people, I have spent weeks in Céret finding the very places in the streets and on the mountainsides where Soutine stood to paint in 1919–20 and 1921, and am none the wiser for it. What Soutine did with Céret is a great mystery and very wonderful.

That afternoon in 1919, when he got off the train 900 kilometres south of Paris and made his way up to the town, he began to learn it without surprise. The streets burdened by heat and dust in which he acquired the habit of resisting the drowsiness of the siesta, and of painting with his back to the trees in the Place de la Liberté. The streets the width of a handcart, the pavé, the marble fountain with 1713 on it in the Place des Neuf Jets. The red roofs began to tug at him. He began to move about with such energy that he could almost have run into himself under the dark almond trees in the square. Subjects moved closer to him. His picture-plane tilted up. The surfaces of the pictures became racked by increasingly convoluted drawing in wet paint, fluid, risky, ecstatic. Designs surged in majestic passages towards the edges of the paintings, especially along the top and towards the right edge, as though in the grip of a strong current. Everything had to come together at once or not at all.

He took a room over a grocer's shop in rue de la République, number 9. He painted the carcasses hanging on the butcher's shop of Monsieur Llarens opposite the house called Casa del Bisbe. Then he tried the path above the Convent des Capucins. There were swarms of swifts on the bell-tower of St-Pierre. Then he had to change his room and lodged for a time at 5 rue Pierre Rameil. He painted the view looking up at the Colline de Céret from Les Tins. He moved again, and had the idea of climbing up through the market gardens below the château so that he could paint the straight street, rue Pierre Brune, from above, showing how it divided the town like a split carcass with red roofs on either side.

Freedom woke in him a particular curiosity. Beyond the town were the cypresses and the simmering air. In the shadows the roads became dark. Smudged people and chairs lodged in the shade as memories. He painted ever faster, making constructive use of difficulties. Marcus Aurelius said that what bars our way, and sometimes prevents work, often turns out to be the work itself. Soutine's solutions became ever more beautiful and original.

He moved to the semi-derelict Hôtel Garreta, in rue Saint-Ferréol, and it was from the little courtyard behind the hotel that a melancholy column of blue smoke went up when he burned many of the Céret pictures which did not please him.

Not long after he returned to Paris he was sitting on a bench, trying not to think about food, when an acquaintance came running and told him to clean up and go to Zborowski's gallery because an American collector was buying his paintings. This was Albert Barnes, a chemicals millionaire who, on this one visit, bought fifty paintings by Soutine – some accounts say many more. From that moment, Soutine did not have to worry about money. Other collectors followed. It is unpleasant to think that Soutine, when he was broke for all those years, had assured acquaintances he would one day repay the money he borrowed from them, but he never did. In fact, he rather avoided them. He moved out of Cité Falguière and bought an apartment, though he never took to washing. At last he could buy food, but his stomach was by this time in such a state that he found he could not eat. He became afraid that meat would rot in his intestines. He refused to use banks, fearing that tellers would strangle him. Photographs show him in smartly cut suits, with an expensive haircut and expensive shoes. His weakness was for trilby hats, of which he bought a great many.

And the paintings? His new circumstances meant that it was now much easier for him to indulge two preferences. One was for buying 18th- and 19th-century pictures which he could paint over, because he liked working on the nap of old canvas. The other was more complicated. When he wanted to paint his own version of earlier masterpieces, he needed not to interpret the subject itself but to set it up afresh. Hence the extraordinary kerfuffle in 1925 when he acquired a beef carcass from the slaughterhouse and hoisted it up in his studio in order to base his own picture on Rembrandt's *Flayed Ox* (1655). He had to bribe the neighbours to let him keep it despite the stench, and refreshed its glistening colour by tipping over it buckets of fresh blood.

In the same way, for his version of Chardin's *The Ray* (1728, Louvre), he reassembled all its elements except the cat in his studio, repeatedly painting the fish with its screaming mouth and dead eyes. At various times there were atrocious difficulties over models, as with the particular woman, Marie, he insisted upon in 1930–31 for his reworkings of Rembrandt's *Woman Bathing in a Stream* (1654), and a girl he considered essential for a reclining figure on a riverbank after Courbet. No one else would do. Her husband, a railway gatekeeper, suspecting Soutine's motives, forbade her to pose. Soutine threatened legal action and eventually the husband was bought off.

Soutine became equally demanding over his choice of subjects in the landscape. He needed to be overwhelmed with enthusiasm, and in the thirties there were long periods when he could find nothing that set him going. There was a particular broken-down horse, some pigs. When he spent the summers of 1930–35 at the château at Lèves, as a guest of his patrons Madeleine and Marcellin Castaing, corners of Chartres gave him what he needed. The shadow across the steps up to the cathedral from rue de Bourg, with a woman and child. And if a picture could have its starting point with reference to a great precedent, so much the better. Corot's painting of the west end of the cathedral, done in 1830 when there was a pile of stone at the foot of rue du Cheval-Blanc, provoked Soutine into at least two masterpieces. Something indescribably beautiful happens when he draws the two quite different spires, the northern one throwing off its flurry of brushstrokes, that are gargoyles, against energetic marks in the sky, and then the whole building, including the rose window, summed up in a sensationally magnificent passage of green and grey, painted, apparently, at one mighty blast. Soutine's ability to sum up the complexities of a whole building in one sweep of passionate brushing is never better shown than in his paintings of Chartres Cathedral. This is what painting can do to the spirit.

He had felt something of the same impulse in 1928–29 when he became fixated with the great plane tree that stands above the wall at Vence. He painted it over and over again. He called it, too, a cathedral.

But now, with Chartres, there was the additional layer of meaning produced by painting something that was already a mighty work of art in its own right. Everything needed to be expressed simultaneously in a gust of imagination, observation and response. As a display of excitable drawing in wet paint, to represent the very essence of what it is like to be human, his paintings of the cathedral are supremely successful. Someone once saw Soutine stamping his foot and cursing in front of the *Jewish Bride*, so astounded was he by the beauty of the paint, its handling, and the impossibility of his ever getting close to Rembrandt's ability to combine brushing with meaning. I dread to think of his exhaustion after long attempts at painting Chartres Cathedral in the hot sun of 1933, long before the general Post Office opposite its south porch became the old Café Serpente. The spires with their punched apertures, the beautiful scraped and rubbed sky, the quickly indicated group of nuns and the two figures standing on a red ground, the spatter of flung paint, the derelict shutters scratched in on the old house below the west front, the red roof and tall chimneys of the priesthouse, the changes of mind, erasures, revisions and sudden insights. The miraculous accuracy of the paint positively causes you to hear the tenor bell and the clatter of pigeons flying suddenly up.

In talking about Soutine's last paintings I need to discuss the idea of risk. Risk in painting is characteristic of many artists' last work, in particular that of Rembrandt, Titian and Soutine. That is because they knew far too much to be held up by technical difficulties and because it no longer mattered to them very much what patrons and buyers might expect. But it was also infinitely more than that. It has to do with something just out of sight, the impulse to make visible something sensed but as yet unrealized which, in this crisis of confusion which is painting, will be a return to simplicity and order. There is a strong suspicion on the part of the painter that this state already exists, that he or she knew it once but has forgotten it, somehow lost touch with it. It stood over his bed when he slept, and over his imagination, but now he cannot grasp it. Working, as he does, on the very edge of intuition, he is used to responding without waiting for explanations.

In Soutine's case, extreme anxiety and angst are part of his method of inner expression turned outwards, his way of making something his own by realizing it in a system of energetic marks. Nietzsche insists that it is necessary to get in touch with one's passions and then submit them to discipline. But this version of self-realization is patently not a discipline. It is more like the terrible freedom and loneliness of Sartre's self-making. To get in touch with your inner genius you act now, this very moment, on impulse and exactly true to your own nature. So the artist, in this turmoil of the psyche, takes risks. He has to. He is not about to reason himself towards a solution, and he knows from experience that a gesture made on impulse, without a rationale, can sometimes embody a truth. This energetic ardour, an uncontrolled appetite for paint and life, can produce out of violence and disorder and profound anarchy an occasional truth, the truth he first imagined, as if by accident.

*

This, in the end, is what great late painting can be: the world reduced to a series of prodigious impulses, the revelation of the inner self intact, the chance taken to see the universe in a new light at the risk of failing utterly.

In the last paintings of Soutine he moves right back from his subject. He is no longer trying to remake old master pictures. He is free. Now there is just him and the paint and the present day. And pain. The subject becomes painting itself. There may be certain things you cannot paint at a particular time. By 1941, Soutine had left the Villa Seurat and was hiding, first in Paris and then in the country, with frequent changes of small towns and villages, because he was a Jew. The mayor of Richelieu, near Tours, supplied him with a false identity card and hid him in the village of Champigny-sur-Veuldre. Soutine felt hunted.

But consider the pictures of two children playing on a log at Champigny in 1942 or '43. It is a beautiful day. Early summer. There is a field of buttercups, dashed in, and three tall poplars. The village roofs and church spire. The children are drawn and redrawn quickly. They are throwing themselves about. They are contorted. At one moment you see their likenesses, their facial features, bare legs and feet. The log is doubled. The blue sky with white in it is brushed with delight onto a brown canvas. With a scribble of drawing in wet paint, Soutine evokes the excitement of the mark and what caused it.

The *process* of painting at a particular moment. Pure painting. Throwing everything in. It still makes him nervous but one idea is as good as another. He fills the space with an attitude. Everything is gesture. He sees how far he can go. He asks himself, 'What am I doing? I did not start like this. I paint of my own free will. Everything is there already.' He floats the paint faster. He wants to put in the small drama of the figures, the houses, just a glimpse of something, the ridiculously beautiful fresh yellow of buttercups as splodges on the green, the ringing blue and white of the sky. Could the children be him and his friend Michel Kikoïne at Smilaviču? There must surely have been a moment when he was happy, excited, young, when the sky was blue, the air clear and he felt no pain.

There is yet time to accomplish something without explanations, just to fill the space with his own free will. And then to stop. Not to make some point, find an answer, solve a problem, come to a conclusion. Just to stop and either keep the painting or destroy it.

No one sees this in the late paintings or makes a case for them. The two little figures sometimes hold hands. They run beneath the trees at Civry. Sometimes the weather is threatening. Sometimes there are poppies. Sometimes the girl is younger and wears a dress. Sometimes the farm-track goes past the children and disappears into the clump of trees. Sometimes there is a wind in the tops of the branches and a single poplar stands separated from the aspen. Towards the end, the girl has grown up and has flopped down in the grass. There is a stretch of peaceful water with reflections. Swans. It is hot. And yet, with France occupied, Soutine is hunted and his stomach is killing him.

In August 1943 an ulcer ruptures and he has an internal haemorrhage. Hiding from the Nazis, he takes too long to get back to Paris, dies on the operating table, is buried in Montparnasse cemetery. Near Baudelaire. What is painting?

Without prejudice, the kitchen wireless, in even tones, told me of the race to the death between vaccines and the plague. It might as well have been reporting stock prices.

Like any other virus, the plague was mutating in cunning ways. Each time a successful vaccine was introduced it changed course to evade it. Each successive variant was quicker to transmit infection than its predecessor, and within three months one appeared from South Africa that sneaked past the human immune system without so much as announcing itself with symptoms. There was an acceleration of deaths worldwide. Vaccines were either stolen or dreadfully slow in distribution.

In Britain, hospitals overflowed and then ran out of oxygen. Emergency calls went unanswered. Mortuaries were unable to deal with the numbers of corpses. In Poland, all available vaccines were commandeered by politicians and celebrities. In Spain there were no nurses, in Greece no needles. Populations began to break laws on quarantine. Exhausted and frightened people refused to be locked down, with terrible consequences. There were food shortages because there was no freight transport. Stations and airports were closed and permanently decommissioned. The United States, which had a higher death rate than anywhere else, went mad; incited by the president, a seditious mob overran the Capitol and broke into the Senate.

And then the old house in winter. The outside, obliterated by snow, buried its conformity to things within. The country of my mind was closed to me. Turning air. Whiteness thickened space. The garden silent and shrunken, the land cold. The days were over as soon as they began. Snow, losing its fingerhold, dropped heavily from impediment to impediment. Ideas slid helpless over edges. Bitter days. Hearts shut in the hard ground. Loss, and growing stiff. The vaccine too late.

One day, I remember, there was a yellow aconite in flower under a lime tree. And I found the shockingly light body of the thrush which had sung in ecstasy all summer. I was dead, but the pictures would remain.

Notes

Page 1
Blake wrote this in an exhibition catalogue of his pictures in 1805. There are other versions. This one was on the wall of a painting studio at the Slade School, London, in the 1950s.

FRANS HALS'S LAST PAINTING
1. Letter to Theo van Gogh. Antwerp, Monday, 28 December 1885.
2. Ibid.
3. Ibid.
4. Letter to Theo van Gogh. Antwerp, Saturday, 28 November 1885.

GWEN JOHN AND ABSENCE
1. National Library of Wales MS 22276A.
2. National Library of Wales MS 22278A.
3. National Library of Wales MS 22287A.
4. National Library of Wales MS 22278A.
5. National Library of Wales MS 22293C.

CLAUDE, POUSSIN AND TIME
Wasps and flying ants:
1. Cézanne.
2. Arp.
3. A. Reynolds.
4. A. Reynolds.
5. Hazlitt.
6. Empson.
7. Mérot.

DAUMIER ON NOT FINISHING
1. This sentence breaks off unfinished.

Acknowledgments

In writing this short book I have been heavily dependent on other people's scholarship. Because I was working from memory and in isolation I used only my books and old exhibition catalogues, which are dog-eared and self-indulgent resources. I have tried to locate some partly inexplicable state of mind in the paintings but someone else had first to provide the facts about them. I have listed those sources I can find and am grateful to their authors. I also apologize to all those whose names and publications I have forgotten, after a lifetime of looking, and inadvertently left out. They belong in the end to hot afternoons in Céret and Bologna and snowy days in Paris when the going was good.

I am indebted to Raymond Queneau's *Exercices de style* (1947). Finally, I have to confess that two famous books lie behind this slight one because on them I had the effrontery to base my idea. They are Henry David Thoreau's *Walden* and Ernest Hemingway's *A Moveable Feast*.

Sources

BONNARD
'Bonnard', in *The Artists of My Life*. Brassaï. Thames & Hudson, 1982
Pierre Bonnard. John Rewald. Museum of Modern Art, New York, 1948

CÉZANNE
Cézanne. John Rewald. Thames & Hudson, 1986
Cézanne: The Late Work. Ed. William Rubin. Thames & Hudson, 1978
Watercolour and Pencil Drawings by Cézanne. Lawrence Gowing.
    Arts Council of Great Britain, 1973

CLAUDE
Claude Lorrain: Liber Veritatis. Michael Kitson. British Museum, 1978

CONSTABLE
Constable. John Walker. Thames & Hudson, 1979
Constable: Masterpieces in Colour. C. Lewis Hind. T. C. Jack, 1907
Constable: Paintings, Drawings and Watercolours. Basil Taylor.
    Phaidon, 1973
Constable: Paintings, Watercolours and Drawings. Tate, 1976
East Bergholt: Constable Country. Ian St John. Suffolk Walkers, 2002
John Constable, 1776–1837. John Lloyd Fraser. Hutchinson, 1976
John Constable's Sketch-Books of 1813 and 1814. Introduction by
    Graham Reynolds. HMSO, 1973
Late Constable. Anne Lyles, Matthew Hargraves. Royal Academy of
    Arts, 2022

DAUMIER
Daumier. Curt Schweicher, trans. Lucy Norton. Heinemann, 1954
Daumier: Paintings and Drawings. Introduction by Alan Bowness.
    Arts Council of Great Britain, 1961
Daumier. Scènes de vie et vies de scène. Electa, 1998
Honoré Daumier, 1808–1879: les dessins d'une comédie humaine.
    Jean-Jacques Lévêque. ACR, 1999

GOYA
Goya. Xavier de Salas. Studio Vista, 1978
Goya: The Witches and Old Women Album. Ed. Juliet Wilson-Bareau and
    Stephanie Buck.Courtauld Gallery, 2015

HALS
Frans Hals: Life, Work and Restoration. Norbert Middelkoop and
  Anne van Grevenstein-Kruse.Uniepers, 1989

JOHN
Gwen John. Mary Taubman. Scolar Press, 1985
Gwen John 1876–1939. Intro. Mary Taubman. Anthony d'Offay, 1976
Gwen John: An Interior Life. Cecily Langdale and David Fraser Jenkins.
  Phaidon, 1985
Gwen John: Letters and Notebooks. Ed. Ceridwen Lloyd-Morgan. Tate, 2004

MICHELANGELO
Michelangelo. Howard Hibbard. Penguin, 1975

POUSSIN
Nicolas Poussin: Masterpieces 1594–1665. Pierre Rosenberg and
  Véronique Damian. Cassell, 1995

REMBRANDT
Rembrandt. Christopher White. Thames & Hudson, 1984
Rembrandt as an Etcher: A Study of the Artist at Work. Christopher White.
  A. Zwemmer, 1969

REYNOLDS
Alan Reynolds: The Making of a Concretist Artist. Michael Harrison.
  Lund Humphries, 2011

ROUAULT
Georges Rouault: The Early Years, 1903–20. Fabrice Hergott,
  Sarah Whitfield. Royal Academy, 1993

SOUTINE
Chaïm Soutine. Introduction by Joanna Drew. Arts Council of
  Great Britain, 1981
Chaïm Soutine. Catalogue raisonné. Maurice Tuchman,
  Esti Dunow, Klaus Perls. Benedikt Taschen Verlag, 1993

TITIAN
Titian: His Life. Sheila Hale. Harper, 2012
Venetian Art: From Bellini to Titian. Johannes Wilde. Oxford, 1974

VELÁZQUEZ
Spanish Painting. Gotthard Jedlicka. Thames & Hudson, 1963
Velázquez' Work and World. José López-Rey. Faber, 1968

List of Illustrations

Dimensions are cited height before width; in cm followed by inches in brackets.

1. Paul Cézanne working on a view of Mont Sainte-Victoire at Les Lauves, 1906. Photo by Print Collector/Getty Images.

2. Paul Cézanne, *The Cathedral at Aix-en-Provence from Les Lauves*, 1902–6. Pencil and watercolour with gouache, 31.8 × 47 (12½ × 18½). Alex Hillman Family Foundation, New York.

3. Brassaï, Pierre Bonnard painting his final four pictures, Le Cannet, 1946. Private Collection. © Estate Brassaï – RMN-Grand Palais, photo © RMN-Grand Palais/Michèle Bellot.

4. Pierre Bonnard, *La Salle à Manger*, 1942–46. Oil on canvas, 83.2 × 100 (32¾ × 39⅜). Private Collection.

5. Titian, *Pietà* (detail), 1575–76. Oil on canvas, 389 × 351 (153 × 138). Accademia, Venice. Photo Scala, Florence – courtesy of the Ministero Beni e Att. Culturali e del Turismo.

6. Michelangelo, *The Crucifixion with the Virgin and St John*, 1550–60. Drawing (black chalk heightened with lead white), 41.3 × 28.6 (16¼ × 28¼). Trustees of the British Museum, London.

7. Rembrandt van Rijn, *Self Portrait*, 1655. Oil on canvas, 53 × 54 (20¾ × 21¼). Bridgewater Collection Loan, Scottish National Gallery, Edinburgh.

8. Rembrandt van Rijn, *The Jewish Bride*, c. 1665–69. Oil on canvas, 121.5 × 166.5 (47¾ × 65½). Rijksmuseum, Amsterdam.

9. Frans Hals, *Lady Regentesses of the Old Men's Almhouse, Haarlem*, c. 1664. Oil on canvas, 249.5 × 170.5 (98¼ × 67). Frans Hals Museum, Haarlem.

10. Camille Pissarro, *L'Église Saint-Jacques à Dieppe*, 1901. Oil on canvas, 54.5 × 65.5 (21½ × 25¾). Musée d'Orsay, Paris. Photo RMN-Grand Palais (Musée d'Orsay)/Hervé Lewandowski.

Index

References in **bold** refer to colour plate sections